EMOTIONAL INTELLIGENCE IN CHRIST STUDY GUIDE

Estella Chavous, EdD
Richard Cummins, MAOL
Lauren E Miller, MEd

EDGE GOD IN PRESS

Copyright ©2023 Dr.Estela Chavous, Rich Cummins, and Lauren E Miller. All rights reserved.

Limit of Liability and Disclaimer of Warranty: The authors and publisher have used their best efforts in preparing this book, and the information provided herein is as is."

No part of this book may be reproduced or transmitted in any form or by any means, electronic or mechanical, including photocopying, recording, or by any information storage or retrieval system, except as may be expressed permitted by law or in writing from the authors, or expert reviewer who may quote brief passages in a review to be printed in a magazine, newspaper, or online website.

Permission should be addressed in writing to eicteam@emotionalintelligenceinChrist.com.

All Scripture quotations, unless otherwise indicated, are taken from the holy bible. New International Version NIV, Copyright @1973, 1978, 1984, 2011 by Biblica Inc. Used by permission of Zondervan. All rights reserved worldwide. www.zondervan.com. The New NIV and New International Version are trademarks registered in the United States Patent and trademark office by Biblica, Inc.

Cover Design and Layout by DocUmeant Designs, www.DocUmeantDesigns.com.

Library of Congress Control Number: 2023902341

ISBN: 978-0-9994172-3-2

Contents

INTRODUCTION v
YOUR PERSONAL IDENTITY IN CHRIST viii

    EIC Study Guide Week 1 - 1

        Day 1: Your Intrinsic Identity   1
        Day 2: Your Intrinsic Purpose   10
        Day 3: How Does God See You?   18
        Day 4: Your Identity in Christ   25
        Day 5: Your Anchored Personal Identity   32

YOUR PERSONAL IDENTITY IN CHRIST 40

    Your Personal Identity in Christ (b) Week 2 - - - - - - - - - - - - 41

        Day 1: Identity Hijacked   41
        Day 2: Identity Restored   49
        Day 3: Jesus's Authority to Set Us Free   56
        Day 4: Choosing Freedom   64
        Day 5: An Undivided Heart   72

SELF-CONTROL 80

    Self-Control (Self-Management) Week 3   - - - - - - - - - - - - - 81

        Day 1: What is Self-Control?   81
        Day 2: Developing Emotional Intelligence   90
        Day 3: Emotional Intelligence + Self-Control = Consistency   98
        Day 4: "Do You Love Me?"   106
        Day 5: Abiding in God's Unconditional Love   113

ALTRUISTIC ATTITUDE 122

    Altruistic Attitude/Social Awareness Week 4 - - - - - - - - - - - 123

        Day 1: Loving Your Neighbor as Yourself   123
        Day 2: Intimacy with God   131
        Day 3: Being in Relationship with Self, Others, and Christ   139
        Day 4: The Christian Ecosystem   147
        Day 5: Appropriate Altruistic Concern   154

CHRIST CONNECTIONS 162

    Christ Connections (Relational Management) Week 5 - - - - 163

        Day 1: Are You Playing the Eternal or Finite Game of Life?   163
        Day 2: Loving One Another   171
        Day 3: Being Present & Interruptible   178

Day 4: Looking for Divine Appointments	186
Day 5: Persevering: Do Not Give Up!	194

REVIEW & REFLECT 204

Review & Reflect Week 6 — 205

Day 1: Look Inside	205
Day 2: Christ Encounters	207
Day 3: Action Items	209
Day 4: Memory Verses	211
Day 5: To Sum It Up	213

EIC STUDY GUIDE CONCLUSION. 215
5 STEPS TO LEAD AN EMOTIONAL INTELLIGENCE IN CHRIST 6-WEEK STUDY GROUP .217
MEET THE EIC TEAM 219

INTRODUCTION

GUIDING BIBLE VERSE

*"Whatever you do,
work at it with all your heart,
as working for the Lord,
not for human masters"*

(Colossians 3:23).

BEFORE YOU BEGIN

Thank you for picking up this *Emotional Intelligence in Christ 6-Week Study Guide!* We are honored that you will be journeying with us through the next six weeks. Our hope is that the reflections, prayers, and exercises in this book will help you grow in your ability to hear and respond to the voice of Christ-within-you.

The journey of Emotional Intelligence in Christ has seven entry points:
- ✞ Emotional Intelligence In Christ Book
- ✞ First Steps In Emotional Intelligence in Christ Course
- ✞ First Steps into Emotional Intelligence in Christ Training
- ✞ Emotional Intelligence in Christ Deep Dive Workshop
- ✞ **Emotional Intelligence in Christ 6-Week Study Guide**
- ✞ Train the Trainer Self-Study and Workshop
- ✞ Emotional Intelligence in Christ Small Group and 1:1 Coaching

You will notice that we pull in quotes from our book: *Emotional Intelligence in Christ (Referenced as EIC throughout this study guide)*, which also contains two self-assessments: Biblical and Emotional Intelligence. If you are interested in diving deeper into how God wired you in your behavior and emotions, you can explore the book and course at: **EmotionalIntelligenceinChrist.com**.

In this 6-week study, we will take you on a journey through the four phases of Emotional Intelligence in Christ and explore personal application:
- ✞ Identity in Christ (Self-Awareness)
- ✞ Self-Control (Self-Management)
- ✞ Altruistic Attitude (Social Awareness)
- ✞ Christ-Connections (Relationship Management)

Before we begin our 6-week journey together, let us briefly summarize and review the Chavous/Cummins/Miller/Voges EIC Method (EIC Method) described in Chapter 8 of The Emotional Intelligence in Christ Book (from here on EIC). Keeping this framework in mind throughout your study will help train you to pause, ask the Holy Spirit for insight and guidance, and adjust your behavior to be Christlike before you respond. We believe that growth in this area will be transformative for you and the church at large.

ENCOUNTER (E)

Remember that the EIC Method defines an Encounter as not just any encounter but rather a God-ordained, predestined encounter that is intentional and by design. Although it can happen anywhere, at any time, and with anyone, it doesn't occur by accident. It was brought into our lives on purpose and it therefore behooves us to *pay attention* to it and be intentional in our response.

IDENTIFIED BEHAVIOR (I)

This phase of the EIC method is the great PAUSE. It is your opportunity to apply all that you are learning in this study. It takes place between the encounter and your actual response to it. Engaging this phase effectively will ensure that you respond thoughtfully out of your identity in Christ rather than simply react (out of your flesh).

> Your ability to pause, consider the tools and insights you have learned in this book and practice listening and following the voice of Christ will equip you to have more profound Christ Connections throughout your day.

During this phase you will *consider*:
1. the other person's personality
2. your own personality
3. each of your motivations

COURSE CORRECT (C)

During this phase of the EIC Method, you will build on your reflections from the Identified Behavior (I) phase and choose to respond with Christ-centered action. It involves three steps: First, surrender to God's will. Second, ask the Holy Spirit to lead you in the right direction, in the right sequence, and at the right speed. And third, having applied each step of the EIC Method, *act* in a way that will bring honor to God.

As we already mentioned, we devised this tool to help you learn to better understand and manage your own emotions and behavior. It takes repetition to build a new habit. After practicing and reflecting on the EIC Method for 42 days, we hope you will have acquired some new habits that will become your natural and instinctive responses in all of your Christ Encounters. Every day over the course of the next 6-weeks we will ask you to reflect on one encounter (E) you had, the behaviors and motivations you were able to identify in yourself and others (I), and the way you decided to respond rather than react (C).

Many blessings to you as you embark on this 6-week journey of increasing your emotional intelligence in Christ.

Connecting Hearts in Him,

Estella, Lauren, and Rich

SUPPORT RESOURCES

Join the EIC Podcast "Edge God In" where we cover *Emotional Intelligence in Christ* and many other topics to Champion Your Human Potential in Christ: **https://EdgeGodIn.com**.

Visit: **https://EmotionalIntelligenceinChrist.com/Videos** to access the video lesson for each week. Each video will give you an introduction to the topics you will explore along with personal testimony, insights and teaching around the phase of *Emotional Intelligence in Christ* you are focusing on that week.

5 Steps to lead an *Emotional Intelligence in Christ 6-Week Study Guide* small group is located at the end of this book, "5 Steps to Lead an Emotional Intelligence in Christ 6-Week Study Group" on page 217.

For a more in-depth facilitator guide please email us at:
EICTeam@emotionalintelligenceinChrist.com.

Intro to Week 1
Your Personal Identity in Christ
(a) (Self-Awareness)

MEMORY VERSE FOR THE WEEK:
"I have been crucified with Christ and I no longer live, but Christ lives in me. The life I now live in the body, I live by faith in the Son of God, who loved me and gave himself for me."
(Galatians 2:20)

A SUPPORT RESOURCE FOR THE WEEK TO EXPLORE

Edge God In Podcast: A 3 Step Prison Break Part 1
https://edgegodin.com/edge-god-in-podcast-23-3-step-prison-break-part-1/

Welcome Message

Welcome, everyone, to this *Emotional Intelligence in Christ 6-Week Study Guide*! We are so glad you are here and pray this will be an enriching time of study, reflection, and transformation for you and the people you walk this journey with.

As you more closely study the identity of Christ and the identity of Christ *in you*, we cannot wait to hear how you, the church, and your community are transformed. Visit us at emotionalintelligenceinchrist.com. Any time we humbly come into the presence of Christ willing to learn, He will honor that desire. Allow yourself to be challenged by the questions and reflection opportunities contained here. Allow yourself to be stretched and to grow. Enjoy this opportunity to intentionally set aside time for spiritual renewal.

Identity is powerful. It is the core of us; the place from which our thinking and our actions spring. It is also the source of so much of our perception. As your awareness of Christ-in-you, the hope of glory, changes and matures, so will your perception of yourself-in-the-world. We are excited to hear of all the ripple effects of blessing this will bring about for you and those entrusted to your care.

Connecting Hearts in Him,

Estella, Lauren, and Rich

EIC STUDY GUIDE WEEK 1

Quote for the Day

"As a follower of Jesus, understanding who I am begins with understanding Whose I am. Who I am is not externally focused, but internally received as a child of God and follower of Jesus. It seems strange to say Whose I am versus Who I am. Because of Jesus, my identity is forever changed to the righteousness of God."
(Phyllis Hendry, co-author of Lead Like Jesus Revisited, as quoted in EIC, p. 44)

Day 1
YOUR INTRINSIC IDENTITY

What God's Word Says

But you are a chosen people, a royal priesthood, a holy nation, God's special possession, that you may declare the praises of him who called you out of darkness into his wonderful light" **(1 Peter 2:9)**.

Pause & Reflect

How would the people who know you best describe you? How would you describe yourself? Who would you say you are?

....
....
....
....
....
....
....
....
....

A PRAYER FOR TODAY

Lord, I commit to you this journey of discovering more fully my identity in you. You made me; you know me completely. You know everything you made me for. As the psalmist declares in Psalm 139:1–6.

> You have searched me, Lord,
>   and you know me.
> You know when I sit and when I rise;
>   you perceive my thoughts from afar.
> You discern my going out and my lying down;
>   you are familiar with all my ways.
> Before a word is on my tongue
>   you, Lord, know it completely.
> You hem me in behind and before,
>   and you lay your hand upon me.
> Such knowledge is too wonderful for me,
>   too lofty for me to attain.

Thank you for this opportunity to learn more about my identity in you. Please help me to know you more, as well. So, I will know Whose I am . . . and therefore walk more fully in who I am.

In Jesus's name,

Amen

Today's Topic
CHRIST IN YOU: THE HOPE OF GLORY

Have you ever wished there was a little more hope in the world? A little more goodness? A little more joy? A little more beauty? Have you ever read or watched the news, sighed a sigh of resignation, and thought to yourself, "Oh Lord, there are so many crazy people out there. Please protect us from all that madness!"?

Well, good news! You're here! Christ is among us; the hope of glory. God wants to bring more hope and joy into the world—through YOU!

When Jesus was faced with a large crowd that had followed him to hear him preach and hadn't eaten for a while, his disciples approached him. They were aware that something had to be done, so they said to Jesus, "This is a remote place, and it's already getting late. Send the crowds away, so they can go to the villages and buy themselves some food." But Jesus replied, "They do not need to go away. *You* give them something to eat." (Matthew 14:15–16, emphasis added)

You give them something to eat. You have the power to make a difference. How could the disciples give thousands of people enough food to eat at that very moment? They were not yet fully aware of the power available to them in Christ, so this task seemed impossible to them. And yet, as we know, it was not impossible for Jesus.

Jesus, the hope of the world, lives in you. He wants to make his appeal to the world through you. He is here. Give him all the room you can in your life and watch him bless the world through you. We promise, it will be an adventure of a lifetime.

What is Jesus telling his disciples in this situation? That their concern isn't valid? That they shouldn't be thinking about the safety and wellbeing of the people they are reaching? That they are not wise to think and plan ahead, especially for the frail, elderly, young, and weak among them who have come to hear Jesus but will need sustenance? Or that it isn't smart to practice preemptive crowd control by making sure everyone is well-fed and comfortable? No, the need is real. But the solution to the problem stretches the disciples' current imaginations.

In order for the disciples to meet the need Jesus is asking them to meet when He says, "You feed them," their understanding of who they are and Whose they are will have to expand. Their faith will have to grow. Much like us, they are not yet living in full awareness of who Christ is; they are still getting to know him. They are not yet living into their full identities in God; they are still discovering them. By inviting them to become the solution to the problem they see, Jesus is inviting them into a deeper knowledge of Him and of their God-given identities. He is inviting them to step out and grow. So that through their faithful service Christ, the hope of glory, would be revealed.

Look Inside

As you reflect on the miraculous feeding of the 5,000, what do you think the disciples took away from this experience of Jesus? How were they changed? Which of the following aspects of their thinking do you think would have been most affected/stretched/challenged by this experience? Which of these would have most stood out to you?

- ☨ Their view of God's love.
- ☨ Their view of Jesus's power.
- ☨ Their view of themselves as followers of Jesus.
- ☨ Their perception of the power of prayer.
- ☨ Something else? ....

Is God asking you to stretch and expand your spiritual imagination? What are some nudges from the Holy Spirit you have dismissed because you have been hyperaware of your own limitations? Ask God to give you the faith to know how to pray. Ask Him if He would like to intervene in a particular situation through you. Make yourself available to be a blessing, however He leads.

Where has God shown up miraculously in your life so far? Have you ever experienced supernatural provision that (far) exceeded your immediate need? What did that produce in you? How did that feel? What did it teach you? How did it change your relationship with God?

....
....
....
....
....
....
....

Is God asking you to do something "impossible"? Is there a Kingdom need you can identify but have no idea how to meet?

Ask God for supernatural intervention/provision now:

_____
_____
_____
_____

TO SUM IT UP

- ✝ Understanding Who you are is inseparable from understanding Whose you are. More fully getting to know God will allow you to more fully get to know yourself-in-Him.
- ✝ As a child of God, God wants to expand your imagination as to what is possible in and through you.
- ✝ The more room you give Christ in your life, the more hope is spread through you into the world. God is making His appeal to the world through Christ-in-you, the hope of glory!

MEDITATION MOMENT

Read the following verse from Ephesians 2:10 aloud: "For we are God's handiwork, created in Christ Jesus to do good works, which God prepared in advance for us to do."

Now make it personal: "For I am God's handiwork, created in Christ Jesus to do good works, which God prepared in advance for me to do."

Now refer to the church universal as you include all Christians worldwide in this proclamation and intercede for the wider body of Christ: "For we are God's handiwork, created in Christ Jesus to do good works, which God prepared in advance for us to do."

Action Items

Read this week's memory verse, (along with the reference where it can be found in Galatians 2:20) three times and manually write it out here:

_____
_____
_____
_____

Write the verse above (Ephesians 2:10) on a small card and place it on your mirror to help you remember both Whose you are and Who you are every single day.

- ✞ The next time you're painfully aware of your own limitations in the face of need, ask God to expand your spiritual imagination. How might He see this moment? What might He be up to? What might He be supernaturally equipping you to do? How might He want to intervene? Ask for faith to be part of the answer.
- ✞ Keep a miracle journal. As you grow in faith and step out in your identity in Christ, watch and take note of the miraculous ways God intervenes and provides in your life. Have it ready, so you can document God's goodness in and through you. Wait in eager expectation for His provision. Be ready to praise and thank Him when He shows up in marvelous, surprising, and life-giving ways.

EIC = ENCOUNTER + IDENTIFIED BEHAVIOR + COURSE CORRECT

Daily EIC Reflection

A Reminder to Readers

At the end of each day during your study guide journey, you will have the opportunity to recall an encounter (E) you had with another person OR yourself where strong negative or positive emotions showed up. After you choose an encounter to focus on, you will then have the opportunity to reflect on the behaviors (I) that showed up as a result of the strong emotions evoked by the encounter. You will be able to reflect on what your motivations may have been as well as the other person's motivations and behaviors. Lastly, you will reflect on the opportunity to course correct (C). Observe if the behaviors that crashed your encounter did not honor God or the person you are created to be in Christ, or perhaps your behaviors did honor God. How well did you respond with the help of the Holy Spirit or what you would have wanted to do differently with the guidance of the Holy Spirit? The purpose of this daily exercise is to increase your high noticing around the moments when your emotions and behaviors block your ability to love others well as Jesus did and anchor the habit of the EIC Method in your life. Two examples are provided here.

- ✞ **E (Encounter with another person)**: Today I encountered a very angry person in the parking lot and they screamed at me for taking their spot.

   I (Identify your emotions and behavior): I was scared and angry and screamed back at them as I defended myself with ugly words and behavior.

C (Course Correct): As I got in my car and drove away, I was shaking and started to pray to ask God's forgiveness for how I reacted to the situation. I invited the Holy Spirit in to show me what I could have done differently to make God recognizable in that moment. I was moved to pray for them which eventually calmed me down.

☦ *E (Encounter with myself)*: I pride myself on getting things done when I say I'm going to do them. Today was so packed I totally forgot to follow up with a colleague who needed some information.

I (Identify my emotions and behavior): Even though my colleague was very understanding, I kept criticizing myself throughout the next day: "how could you forget to follow up on that request?" The self-critical thoughts fueled behavior that showed up in other encounters throughout the day, I felt impatient and agitated.

C (Course Correct): As I reflected on my day with the Lord, I invited Him into my negative self-talk which resulted in ugly behavior. He reminded me that I can't give out to others what I don't first receive within from Him. I read scriptures that spoke to how God forgives me and loves me which moved me to begin the next day remembering my worth and value in Jesus. This was a huge course correction for me: anchoring my identity on what God thinks of me verses what I think of me. I carried this with me which resulted in strong positive emotions and behaviors throughout the next day. My EIC Reflection was much different at the end of that day.

Dear reader, earmark this page for future reference to help bring clarity as you work through your daily EIC Reflections.

ENCOUNTER (E)

Describe one Christ Encounter you had today on the lines below. What happened? Where were you? Whom did you encounter? If you're not sure which one to choose, ask the Holy Spirit to highlight one God-ordained Encounter for you.

_____
_____
_____
_____
_____
_____
_____
_____
_____
_____

IDENTIFIED BEHAVIOR (I)

What behaviors did you act out? Drawing on your newfound understanding in today's lesson, which of your own personality traits and motivations were at play? What were the other person's personality traits and motivations that influenced the encounter? Describe them here.

My unique personality traits and motivations:

_____
_____
_____
_____
_____

The other person's unique personality traits and motivations:

_____
_____
_____
_____
_____
_____

How did these distinct traits and motivations interact with each other? Was there a clash? Did they complement each other? Reflect on this below:

COURSE CORRECT (C)

How did you respond? On a Spirit scale from 1–10, how did you do? Were you able to thoughtfully respond rather than react? Did you successfully surrender to God's will and course correct before you took action? Is there anything you wish you had done differently? Remember that we are going for *progress over perfection*. We are all here to learn and grow. Which lessons would you like to take with you going forward? What did you learn? Reflect on your answers to these questions below.

Quote for the Day

"Know this, Satan is consistently prowling around trying to hijack your identity and the authority of God in your life." (EIC, p. 57)

"Once you have given Jesus the authority over your identity in life, you reconnect to the presence of God's love and purpose for you." (EIC, p. 50)

Day 2
YOUR INTRINSIC PURPOSE

What God's Word Says

"We are therefore Christ's ambassadors, as though God were making his appeal through us. We implore you on Christ's behalf: Be reconciled to God. God made him who had no sin to be sin for us, so that in him we might become the righteousness of God" **(2 Corinthians 5:20–21)**.

Pause & Reflect

On a scale from 1 to 10, how in touch are you with your purpose in life? Can you sum it up in a few short sentences? Have you written your own personal mission statement yet? If so, write it out on the lines below. If not, start brainstorming impressions and ideas that may help you write one now.

_____

_____

_____

_____

_____

_____

_____

_____

_____

A PRAYER FOR TODAY:

Lord, thank you that I get to be your child. Thank you for adopting me into your family and calling me your own. Thank you for the privilege of knowing you. And thank you for the purpose you placed in me long before I was able to plan and scheme myself. Help me live into your vision for my life, please.

From before I was born, you have known me. as the Psalmist exclaims in Psalm 139:13–14:

> *For you created my inmost being;*
>   *you knit me together in my mother's womb.*
> *I praise you because I am fearfully and wonderfully made;*
>   *your works are wonderful,*
>   *I know that full well.*

Thank you also for the amazing authority you have given Christ-in-me. Please help me to be faithful to you, so that by your grace I will overcome and be able to fulfill your purpose for me.

In Jesus's name,

Amen

Today's Topic
WALKING IN PURPOSE AND AUTHORITY

What does authority have to do with purpose? Well, in order to live out our God-given purpose in the midst of all the challenges, obstacles, distractions, temptations, and discouragements that come our way, we will have to walk in our God-given authority. We will need power to overcome. There is no way our purpose will not be challenged; we cannot persevere in our own strength. Alone, we are weak in faith, timid, frantically glancing to the left and the right, as Peter did when he was about to drown.

Jesus walked faithfully in his purpose and authority. He knew exactly who He was and He remained obedient until the end. When He spoke, the crowds listened, because "he taught them as one who had authority" (Mark 1:22). Just before Christ ascended to be with the Father, his final words were, "All authority in heaven and on earth has been given to me." (Matthew 28:18) These words are followed by the Great Commission, our ultimate purpose and calling as followers of Christ. Without Christ's authority, however, it is impossible for us to carry it out.

Thankfully and amazingly, Jesus has given us the power and the authority to fulfill his command. In Him, we can overcome every trial and temptation. In Him, we can fulfill our God-ordained purpose. In Him and with the strength of the Holy Spirit, we can remain faithful to the end.

The impossible is made possible because Christ is *in* us. By remaining in Christ, we will be able to fulfill our ultimate purpose. Because we are in Christ, we can be confident that "he who began a good work in [us] will carry it on to completion until the day of Christ Jesus." (Philippians 1:6, adapted)

In Christ, our purpose and our identity are secure.

Look Inside

How comfortable are you with the idea that you have been given spiritual authority to fulfill your purpose?
- ✝ Super comfortable, I walk in it every day!
- ✝ I don't know. It feels a bit preposterous to say that about myself.
- ✝ That makes me uncomfortable. Isn't a follower of Christ supposed to be humble, meek, and mild?

Day 2 Your Intrinsic Purpose

Can you think of anyone you know who walks in authority in a way you admire? What is it about them you respect so much? Can you put it into words? How would you describe them?

_____
_____
_____
_____
_____
_____

If you were to sum up your purpose in one sentence, what would it be?

_____
_____
_____
_____

Please complete the following sentences:

When I am walking in my purpose, I am . . .

When I am walking in my purpose, I feel . . .

When I am walking in my purpose, I think . . .

When I am walking in my purpose, I look . . .

When I am walking in my purpose, I know . . .

TO SUM IT UP

- ✝ In order to faithfully fulfill your purpose, you need to walk in your spiritual authority in Christ.
- ✝ Both you and your purpose are fully known by God (He authored them).
- ✝ As followers of Christ, our ultimate purpose is to fulfill The Great Commission (Read Matthew 28:16–20). But without Christ's authority, it is impossible for us to carry it out.
- ✝ In Christ, we can fulfill our God-ordained purpose.
- ✝ Because of Christ, our purpose and our identity are secure.

Meditation Moment

What are some trials and temptations that have distracted you from your purpose? Can you identify and name them?

_____

Which tools can you use to help you persevere, be faithful, and overcome? Who might be able to support you?

_____

Action Items

- ✝ Read this week's memory verse, (Galatians 2:20) out loud three times, each time trying to commit more of it to memory. Think about what it means and why each of the words were chosen when it was originally written. Create any memory aids you can think of. Rather than read it in print, read your own handwritten version (from yesterday) to help you memorize it.
- ✝ If your personal mission statement (see Pause & Reflect) is not yet fully articulated, complete it. If it is, print (or write) it out and place it somewhere you can see it every day.
- ✝ Choose two of the items you listed under tools (see Meditation Moment) and practice them every day for seven days. How are they affecting you? Reflect on this in your journal every day.
- ✝ Find someone who walks in their spiritual authority in a way you admire (see Look Inside). Ask them to coffee and interview them on what gives them such confidence. What are some of their spiritual practices? What is their view of spiritual authority? Was it always this way for them? Where do they draw their strength?
- ✝ Practice your spiritual authority in Christ in your daily life. When trials and temptations come your way, rebuke them in the name of Jesus and step forward in the confidence He gives you. Rely on the word of God and the Holy Spirit to equip you for every good work.

EIC = ENCOUNTER + IDENTIFIED BEHAVIOR + COURSE CORRECT

Daily EIC Reflection

ENCOUNTER (E)

Describe one Christ Encounter you had today on the lines below. What happened? Where were you? Whom did you encounter? If you're not sure which one to choose, ask the Holy Spirit to highlight one God-ordained Encounter for you.

_____
_____
_____
_____
_____

IDENTIFIED BEHAVIOR (I)

What behaviors did you act out? Drawing on your newfound understanding in today's lesson, which of your own personality traits and motivations were at play?

_____
_____
_____
_____
_____
_____
_____
_____
_____

What were the other person's personality traits and motivations that influenced the encounter? Describe them here:

_____
_____
_____
_____

My unique personality traits and motivations:

The other person's unique personality traits and motivations:

How did these distinct traits and motivations interact with each other? Was there a clash? Did they complement each other? Reflect on this below:

Day 2 Your Intrinsic Purpose

COURSE CORRECT (C)

How did you respond? On a Spirit scale from 1–10, how did you do? Were you able to thoughtfully respond rather than react? Did you successfully surrender to God's will and course correct before you took action? Is there anything you wish you had done differently? Remember that we are going for *progress over perfection*. We are all here to learn and grow. Which lessons would you like to take with you going forward? What did you learn? Reflect on your answers to these questions below:

1 2 3 4 5 6 7 8 9 10

Quote for the Day

"Because of Jesus, my identity is forever changed to the righteousness of God." (Phyllis Hendry, co-author of Lead Like Jesus Revisited, as quoted in EIC, p. 44)

*"Remember, the world screams for your identity. God whispers and invites you to remember **Whose you are, why you are here,** and **why your presence on earth matters.**"* (EIC, p. 52)

DAY 3
HOW DOES GOD SEE YOU?

What God's Word Says

"The Lord does not look at the things that people look at. People look at the outer appearance, but the Lord looks at the heart" **(1 Samuel 16:7).**

"Praise be to the God and Father of our Lord Jesus Christ, who has blessed us in heavenly realms with every spiritual blessing in Christ. For he chose us in him before the creation of the world to be holy and blameless in his sight. In love he predestined us for adoption to sonship through Jesus Christ, in accordance with his pleasure and will—to the praise of his glorious grace, which he has freely given us in the One he loves. In him we have redemption through his blood, the forgiveness of sins, in accordance with the riches of God's grace that he lavished on us" **(Ephesians 1:3–8).**

Pause & Reflect

How do you think God sees you? In the space below, write at least five ways God sees you or five attributes you think God sees in you.

....

....

....

....

....

A PRAYER FOR TODAY

God, your love for me humbles me. I am not worthy that you should call me your child, and yet you do. You look at me with love, kindness, forgiveness, and grace. You see the truest version of me; you know where I come from and where I'm going. You see through all self-deception, all pretense, and every effort to cover up and hide.

Your embrace of me is undeserved and yet it is complete. This is hard for me to grasp. Please help me to let your love that is unlike any other love, in completely. Please transform me by your love.

In Jesus's name,

Amen

Today's Topic
THE GOGGLES OF GOD

When God looks at you, what does he see? What is his lens through which he perceives the reality of who you are? When we think about someone we love, the way we see them may vary day by day. Our perspective may be skewed by our emotional state, our mood, how well we've slept, what we ate, our most recent conversation, any unresolved conflict we might have, or any number of other factors. It may also be influenced by a sense of hope, a vivid imagination, or wishful thinking.

Not so with God. His perspective is absolutely true. He doesn't need to ignore parts of us to love all of us; he knows it all—past, present, and future. His knowledge of us is deeper and more profound than we can grasp. It's pregnant with everything that is yet to come and everything he is still shaping in us.

One of the most beautiful pictures of God in Scripture can be found in the Parable of the Prodigal Son. God, the Father, is depicted as generous, forgiving, and embracing. Why does he treat his prodigal son like that? Why lavish such love on him after everything he had done? Had he not squandered his father's wealth, smeared his father's reputation, and shamed his family? The answer is staggering. The father saw him as worthy. **Worthy.** Even when the prodigal son did not perceive himself as such, in his father's eyes, he was.

When God looks at us and sees Christ-in-us, his beloved Son, who is "crowned with glory and honor" (Hebrews 2:9) and of whom thousands of angels proclaim,

> Worthy is the Lamb, who was slain,
>   to receive power and wealth and wisdom and strength
>   and honor and glory and praise! (Revelation 5:12).

as mind-boggling as it may be, he sees us as that worthy daughter or son. In his eyes we are worthy of adoption, worthy of belonging in his family, worthy of extending himself to reach us, worthy of throwing a party when we come home, worthy of celebrating when we've arrived. What a profound honor to have been included in such an amazing family and to be welcomed with such a joyful, exuberant embrace!

Look Inside

- ✞ How easy is it for you to see yourself as worthy of God's love?
- ✞ Oh yes, it's natural

Day 3 How Does God See You?

- ✟ Depends on the day
- ✟ To be honest, it's tough.
- ✟ Impossible

Has anyone ever treated you with such unexpected kindness that it took your breath away? Please reflect on that moment below. What was so meaningful about it? How has it shaped you?

_____
_____
_____
_____
_____
_____
_____
_____

If you could see yourself the way God sees you . . .

How would you feel about yourself?

1. _____
2. _____
3. _____

How would you treat yourself?

1. _____
2. _____
3. _____

How would you treat others?

1. _____
2. _____
3. _____

To Sum It Up

- ✝ Because Christ is worthy of all glory and honor and praise and we are hidden in Him, God sees us as worthy of adoption into His family.
- ✝ God is a loving Father, who welcomes us with His arms outstretched wide.
- ✝ Seeing ourselves the way God sees us transforms us from the inside out.
- ✝ When God looks at you through his "goggles", he sees the righteousness of Christ.

Meditation Moment

Please insert your name in the passage (adapted from Isaiah 43:1–2) below. Then read it to a friend, filling the blank spaces with their name. When you're finished, have them speak the same passage over you (filling in your name). What image does it bring up for you? How does it make you feel? Talk with the Lord about this.

Do not fear, _____, for I have redeemed you; I have summoned you by name; you are mine. When you pass through the waters, I will be with you; and when you pass through the rivers, they will not sweep over you. When you walk through the fire, _____, you will not be burned; the flames will not set you ablaze. For I am the Lord your God, the Holy One of Israel, your Savior.

Action Items

- ✝ Record this week's memory verse on your phone (any voice recording app will do) in your own voice and listen to it three times throughout your day. Speak slowly as you record. As you listen to the recording, try following along with your own recorded voice.
- ✝ The next time you find yourself beating yourself up with negative self-talk, stop yourself and ask God to help you put on His "goggles." How does He see you *right now*, in the midst of your disappointment/anger/disillusion? Ask Him to help you see yourself as He sees you too.
- ✝ Go back to the ways God sees you in the Pause & Reflect exercise "Pause & Reflect" on page 18. Every day this week, stand in front of the mirror and say those attributes to yourself out loud. Declare, "I am . . ." Agree with God on those things!
- ✝ Spend some time in worship and adoration of Jesus, the One who is truly worthy of all glory, honor, and praise.

EIC = ENCOUNTER + IDENTIFIED BEHAVIOR + COURSE CORRECT

Daily EIC Reflection

ENCOUNTER (E)

Describe one Christ Encounter you had today on the lines below. What happened? Where were you? Whom did you encounter? If you're not sure which one to choose, ask the Holy Spirit to highlight one God-ordained Encounter for you.

IDENTIFIED BEHAVIOR (I)

What behaviors did you act out? Drawing on your newfound understanding in today's lesson, which of your own personality traits and motivations were at play? What were the other person's personality traits and motivations that influenced the encounter? Describe them here:

My unique personality traits and motivations:

The other person's unique personality traits and motivations:

How did these distinct traits and motivations interact with each other? Was there a clash? Did they complement each other? Reflect on this below:

COURSE CORRECT (C)

How did you respond? On a Spirit scale from 1–10, how did you do? Were you able to thoughtfully respond rather than react? Did you successfully surrender to God's will and course correct before you took action? Is there anything you wish you had done differently?

Remember that we are going for *progress over perfection*. We are all here to learn and grow. Which lessons would you like to take with you going forward? What did you learn? Reflect on your answers to these questions below:

Quote for the Day

"Scripture is full of descriptors of our identity: Dearly loved (Colossians 3:12), forgiven (Romans 4:7), chosen (John 15:9), a royal priesthood (1 Peter 2:9), the apple of God's eye (Psalm 17:8), the light of the world (Matthew 5:14), heir with Jesus (Romans 8:17), friends (John 15:14) and many more." (Phyllis Hendry, co-author of Lead Like Jesus Revisited, as quoted in EIC, p. 44)

"Are you ready for the journey back to yourself as connected to Christ?" (EIC, p. 46)

Day 4
YOUR IDENTITY IN CHRIST

What God's Word Says

"Yet to all who did receive him, to those who believed in his name, he gave the right to become children of God—children born not of natural descent, nor of human decision or a husband's will, but born of God" **(John 1:12–13)**.

"Therefore, as God's chosen people, holy and dearly loved, clothe yourselves with compassion, kindness, humility, gentleness and patience" **(Colossians 3:12)**.

"Set your minds on things above, not on earthly things. For you died, and your life is now hidden with Christ in God" **(Colossians 3:2–3)**.

Pause & Reflect

Who or what do you love most dearly? What would you do to save it/them from certain destruction?

A PRAYER FOR TODAY

God, the love you have for your Son and the bond you have with Him is unbroken, everlasting, powerful. Not even death could break it. Please help me to understand what it means that I am hidden in Him. Please help me to grasp the height and depth of your love for Christ and the fact that I am included in that love. Please let Paul's words ring true in my life and in the life of my faith community. Strengthen us with the power of your Spirit, root and establish us in Christ's love, and fill us, God, with the fullness of you.

> Ephesians 3:14–19: "For this reason I kneel before the Father, from whom every family in heaven and on earth derives its name. I pray that out of his glorious riches he may strengthen you with power through his Spirit in your inner being, so that Christ may dwell in your hearts through faith. And I pray that you, being rooted and established in love, may have power, together with all the Lord's holy people, to grasp how wide and long and high and deep is the love of Christ, and to know this love that surpasses knowledge—that you may be filled to the measure of all the fullness of God."

In Jesus's name,

Amen

Today's Topic
HOLY AND DEARLY LOVED

"Dearly beloved," this famous phrase begins many an (awkward) depiction of a church gathering in movies, especially weddings. Dearly beloved. We hear it, we smile, we know the scene is being shot in a Christian church service. All because the attendees are being referred to as "beloved!"

To be beloved is a marvelous thing. It means we're special, precious, cared for, considered, included, nurtured, and seen. In Colossians 3:12 we are admonished to clothe ourselves with "compassion, kindness, humility, gentleness and patience" not because we are so "good" but simply because of our identity as holy and dearly beloved children. Because of who we are (God's chosen people), we are to act accordingly. These attributes are a natural overflow of us operating in our true identity.

When we are operating out of our true identity in Christ, we are "unflappable." We are not as easily manipulated, controlled, devastated, hurt, or cast aside. No matter our outer circumstances, we can stand firm. That is because our identity as holy and dearly beloved comes from a realm beyond our own; it is truer than our immediate circumstances and goes deeper than what we can see. Because we are in Christ, it is immutable.

How difficult it can be to remember this when the pressure is on and our lives seem to be falling apart! How difficult it can be to gain the proper perspective, remember what is ultimately true about us, no matter how things appear. That is when we need to put on the mind of Christ and allow Him to teach us.

God doesn't ask us to embody compassion, kindness, humility, gentleness, and patience out of our own strength or by our own sheer willpower. How could we? Our own capacity for these traits is most certainly limited. Instead, he asks us to operate out of our identity in Him and draw from His endless reserves. When we do that, there is a lightness, joy, and simplicity to it—we are simply operating out of who we already are in Him.

Look Inside and Reflect

What does it mean *to you* to be hidden with Christ in God (Colossians 3:3)? How would you explain it to a friend? Put it in your own words.

....

....

....

Being "hidden in" and "dearly loved" all bring up images of warmth, closeness, and intimacy with God. On a scale from 1 to 10, how close would you say you are with God? How aware are you of your belovedness today?

If you were able to remain in God's-love-for-you for a full 24 hours and live only out of your identity in Christ, what do you think would happen? How would you feel/think/act? What would that day be like?

To Sum It Up

- ✞ You are hidden with Christ in God.
- ✞ When you are operating out of who you truly are in Christ, there is a lightness, a joy, and an ease to it. You don't have to force kindness and compassion; they flow through you naturally.
- ✞ The firmer your grasp on your true identity in Christ, the more "unflappable" you become.

Meditation Moment

Return to Ephesians 3:14–19 and insert your own name in the Scripture passage, reading it back to God as a prayer:

For this reason I, _____, kneel before you, Father, from whom every family in heaven and on earth derives its name. Out of your glorious riches, please strengthen me with your power through your Spirit in my inner being, so that you Christ may dwell in my heart through faith. Please root and establish me in love, and give me the power to, together with all of your holy people, grasp how wide and long and high and deep your love is, and know this love that surpasses knowledge—and be filled to the measure of all the fullness of you.

In Jesus's name,

Amen

> ## Action Items
>
> ✞ Listen to your recording of this week's Bible verse again. Now try reciting it from memory (without the recording). Can you do it? Don't forget to quote the reference. Keep practicing it until you feel confident.
>
> ✞ For the next three days, don't get out of bed until you have gotten in touch with the fact that you are beloved of God. Let God love on you. Don't step out into the world before you have gotten in touch with the confidence this truth about your true identity gives you. Be filled with the fullness of God.
>
> ✞ How might God want to love the world through you today? As you go about your day, look for ways to enact your belovedness, to be true to your identity. How? By clothing yourself with "compassion, kindness, humility, gentleness and patience." (Colossians 3:12)
>
> ✞ If God was writing you a love letter, what would he write to you personally? What does God want you to know about your identity in Christ? Take some time to pray, listen, and write down what you hear.

EIC = ENCOUNTER + IDENTIFIED BEHAVIOR + COURSE CORRECT

Daily EIC Reflection

ENCOUNTER (E)

Describe one Christ Encounter you had today on the lines below. What happened? Where were you? Whom did you encounter? If you're not sure which one to choose, ask the Holy Spirit to highlight one God-ordained Encounter for you.

....
....
....
....
....

IDENTIFIED BEHAVIOR (I)

What behaviors did you act out? Drawing on your newfound understanding in today's lesson, which of your own personality traits and motivations were at play? What were the other person's personality traits and motivations that influenced the encounter? Describe them here:

My unique personality traits and motivations:

The other person's unique personality traits and motivations:

How did these distinct traits and motivations interact with each other? Was there a clash? Did they complement each other? Reflect on this below:

COURSE CORRECT (C)

How did you respond? On a Spirit scale from 1–10, how did you do? Were you able to thoughtfully respond rather than react? Did you successfully surrender to God's will and course correct before you took action? Is there anything you wish you had done differently?

Remember that we are going for *progress over perfection*. We are all here to learn and grow. Which lessons would you like to take with you going forward? What did you learn? Reflect on your answers to these questions below:

| 1 | 2 | 3 | 4 | 5 | 6 | 7 | 8 | 9 | 10 |

....
....
....
....
....

Quote for the Day

"Jesus entered into Thomas's lack of faith and trust and pulled Thomas in, through, and out of his doubt. The result: Resurrected conviction and faith along with an anchored personal identity in Christ." (EIC, p. 58)

Day 5
YOUR ANCHORED PERSONAL IDENTITY

What God's Word Says

"We have this hope as an anchor for the soul, firm and secure. It enters the inner sanctuary behind the curtain, where our forerunner, Jesus, has entered on our behalf. He has become a high priest forever, in the order of Melchizedek" **(Hebrews 6:19–20).**

"For this reason I kneel before the Father, from whom every family in heaven and on earth derives its name. I pray that out of his glorious riches he may strengthen you with power through his Spirit in your inner being, so that Christ may dwell in your hearts through faith. And I pray that you, **being rooted and established** in love, may have power, together with all the Lord's holy people, to grasp how wide and long and high and deep is the love of Christ, and to know this love that surpasses knowledge—that you may be filled to the measure of all the fullness of God" **(Ephesians 3:14–19, emphasis added).**

Pause & Reflect

On a scale from 1 to 10, how firmly anchored do you feel in your identity in Christ today?

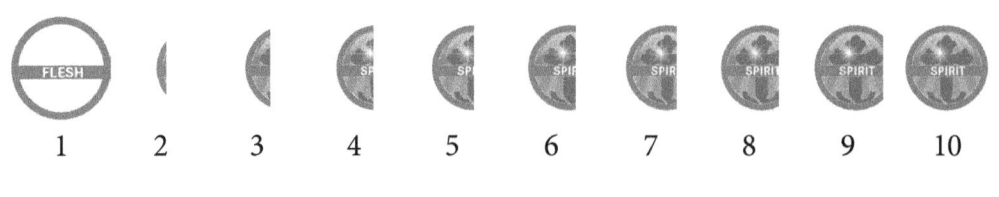

1   2   3   4   5   6   7   8   9   10

....

....

....

....

A PRAYER FOR TODAY

Lord, please anchor my identity in you today. Some days I feel really clear on who I am in you. And other days I flounder, drift, lose perspective, lose confidence, and lose my way. Please anchor me in your truth, please anchor me in your love, and please anchor me in your grace.

In Jesus's name,

Amen

Today's Topic
AN ANCHOR FOR THE SOUL: FIRM AND SECURE

Throughout the Bible, permanence and impermanence are contrasted with one another. Names are written in the book of life, which is then sealed—a sign of permanence. The wicked are like chaff, which the wind blows away—indicating their impermanence. God's love endures forever but mortals are like fleeting shadows; they do not endure. God's promises never fail but the mouth of a fool invites ruin.

In our spiritual lives we experience both permanence and impermanence as well. In the Parable of the Sower (see Matthew 13), Jesus warns us that not all seed that is sown will sprout, grow roots, grow up healthfully, and yield a harvest. Not every effort for the Kingdom of God will produce fruit that will last. Likewise, in the Parable of the Sheep and the Goats (see Matthew 25) and in the sermon recorded in Matthew 7, we are told that not everyone who says, "Lord, Lord" will enter the kingdom of heaven. Whether the rejected disciples were false from the beginning or eventually fell away, we don't know.

Either way, we are encouraged to "stand firm and hold fast to the teachings we passed on to you." We are to "keep God's commands and hold fast [to our] testimony about Jesus." But . . . in this tumultuous life, standing firm and holding fast isn't always easy to do. Sometimes we need something to hold on to us. What might that be? What anchors us in the storms? According to Hebrews 6, it is the hope we have in God's promises.

Throughout the Bible, God makes promises, commitments, and covenants with his people. And He has always proven to be true to His word. His promises are reliable and trustworthy because that's who He is. Because we're not used to such goodness and consistency, they are healing and restorative to us. When everything in our lives is turned upside down and we need something solid, reliable, firm, and unchanging to rely on, God's promises are a good place to go. They can anchor our souls.

Don't know which promise to start with? There are countless promises in God's word to ponder, but here's one to get you started:

> Give thanks to the Lord, for he is good;
> his love endures forever. (Psalm 118:1)

Look Inside

When you reflect on your week, which people/events/practices/things helped you remember God's promises to you? Which people/events/practices/things anchored your soul in Him?

_____
_____
_____
_____
_____

When you reflect on your week, what were the things that caused you to drift or made you lose touch with your true identity in God? What tripped you up? Which events can you identify?

_____
_____
_____
_____
_____

When you reflect on your life, can you recognize a pattern? Are there certain things that trip you up over and over and make you lose touch with or forget your identity in Christ? Please circle the three you struggle with most (or add your own). When you have finished circling the items you most resonate with, write the opposite of each item beside it.

Struggle	Opposite	Struggle	Opposite
Fear		Hopelessness	
Anxiety		Despair	
Worry		Disillusionment	
Confusion		Bitterness	
Isolation		Anger	
Discouragement		Overwhelm	
Grief		Unforgiveness	
Sadness		Loss	
Success		Intimidation	
Overconfidence		Fame	
Wealth		Attention	
Jealousy		Recognition	
Greed		Promotion	
_____		_____	

One of the ways we can remain firmly and securely anchored in God's promises to us is by not forgetting them. But how easily we forget who we are, all God has promised us, and all God has already done in our lives! In Psalm 103:1–5 the psalmist reminds himself intentionally of who God is. He doesn't want his soul to forget; he knows how important it is to remind his soul of the nature of the God in whom it finds its anchor and its home.

> Praise the Lord, my soul;
>   all my inmost being, praise his holy name.
> Praise the Lord, my soul,
>   and forget not all his benefits—
> who forgives all your sins
>   and heals all your diseases,
> who redeems your life from the pit
>   and crowns you with love and compassion,
> who satisfies your desires with good things
>   so that your youth is renewed like the eagle's.

What would you like to remind your soul of? Who has God been for you? What do you want to make sure your soul never forgets? Write it down here.

....
....
....
....

To Sum It Up

- ✝ God's promises anchor our souls.
- ✝ No matter what happens in our lives, we know that God's love endures forever. (Psalm 118:1)
- ✝ Remembering all God is and all God has done in our lives can help us remain firmly anchored in our identity in Him.
- ✝ Because it is so important to remember who and Whose we are, it's a good idea to intentionally practice remembering.

Day 5 Your Anchored Personal Identity

Meditation Moment

Take a look at the three "tripper uppers" you circled under *Look Inside*. Now ponder their opposites. What does the Lord want to teach you about these opposite characteristics? What would your life look like if you were anchored in these positive traits? If they became a firm and permanent part of your personality?

_____
_____
_____
_____
_____

Action Items

✝ Write this week's Bible verse out from memory on the lines below. Don't cheat! Once you have written it out and reviewed it, go back and check it with your handwritten original. How did you do?

_____
_____
_____
_____
_____
_____

✝ Listen to "My Soul's Been Anchored" on YouTube, arranged by Moses Hogan.[1]
✝ The next time you are experiencing one of your personal "tripper uppers" (see Look Inside) and sense yourself feeling a bit adrift spiritually, meditate on the opposite word you wrote down beside that item. Then ask God to fill your heart with it.
✝ Share one item you never want your soul to forget about God with a trusted friend. Listen to them share what they don't want their soul to forget too.
✝ Memorize Psalm 118:1

> Give thanks to the Lord, for he is good;
> his love endures forever.

EIC = ENCOUNTER + IDENTIFIED BEHAVIOR + COURSE CORRECT

Daily EIC Reflection

ENCOUNTER (E)

Describe one Christ Encounter you had today on the lines below. What happened? Where were you? Whom did you encounter? If you're not sure which one to choose, ask the Holy Spirit to highlight one God-ordained Encounter for you.

....
....
....
....
....
....

IDENTIFIED BEHAVIOR (I)

What behaviors did you act out? Drawing on your newfound understanding in today's lesson, which of your own personality traits and motivations were at play? What were the other person's personality traits and motivations that influenced the encounter? Describe them here:

My unique personality traits and motivations:

....
....
....
....

The other person's unique personality traits and motivations:

....
....
....
....

How did these distinct traits and motivations interact with each other? Was there a clash? Did they complement each other? Reflect on this below:

....
....
....
....

COURSE CORRECT (C)

How did you respond? On a Spirit scale from 1–10, how did you do? Were you able to thoughtfully respond rather than react?

Did you successfully surrender to God's will and course correct before you took action? Is there anything you wish you had done differently? Remember that we are going for *progress over perfection*. We are all here to learn and grow. Which lessons would you like to take with you going forward? What did you learn? Reflect on your answers to these questions below:

| 1 | 2 | 3 | 4 | 5 | 6 | 7 | 8 | 9 | 10 |

....
....
....
....
....
....
....

Endnotes

1   The Moses Hogan Singers. "My Soul's Been Anchored." Arranged by Moses Hogan. Accessed December 30, 2022. https://www.youtube.com/watch?v=eYWvenCO5CA

Intro to Week 2
Your Personal Identity in Christ
(b) (Identity Hijacked)

MEMORY VERSE FOR THE WEEK:
"But you are a chosen people, a royal priesthood, a holy nation, God's special possession, that you may declare the praises of him who called you out of darkness into his wonderful light" (1 Peter 2:9).

A SUPPORT RESOURCE
FOR THE WEEK TO EXPLORE
Edge God In Podcast:
Emotional Intelligence in God Step 1
https://edgegodin.com/emotional-intelligence-in-God-step-1

Welcome Message

Welcome to Week 2, where we will continue to delve deeper into our identity in Christ!

Because identity is powerful and complex, there is a lot to explore. Sometimes our identity gets temporarily undermined, distracted, stolen, or buried. We use the word "hijacked" to describe this experience. This week we will explore not only this painful experience but also the hopeful experience of an identity restored. Then we will meditate on Jesus's power and authority to set us free. After that we will focus on freedom as a choice and finally, we will dwell on loving God with our whole, undivided heart.

As we've said before, please engage this process as deeply as possible. Just like any program or tool, you get out of it what you put into it. Allow yourself to be challenged by the questions and reflection opportunities contained here. Allow yourself to be stretched and grow. Enjoy this opportunity to intentionally set aside time for spiritual renewal.

We hope this week's study will encourage you to lean more into your true identity in Christ.

Connecting Hearts in Him,

Estella, Lauren, and Rich

YOUR PERSONAL IDENTITY IN CHRIST (B) WEEK 2

Quote for the Day

"Jesus is the perfect One for us to follow when it comes to establishing our personal identity in God for victory over the world and its desires. Jesus died to all that the world offered in order to save our souls. When he walked this earth, he was on a mission to restore lost identities that had been hijacked by the things that Satan attempted to tempt him with in the desert (Luke 4:1–13): passion, possessions, popularity, and power. Jesus is still on a mission to restore lost identities. Perhaps it's yours that he is after?" (EIC, p. 45)

"Know this, Satan is consistently prowling around, trying to hijack your identity and the authority of God in your life." (EIC, p. 57)

"My coaching question to you, dear reader, is this: what have you allowed to hijack your identity? The drug of approval? The disease to please? The need to be right? Liked? Understood?" (EIC, p. 59)

Day 1
IDENTITY HIJACKED

What God's Word Says

"It is for freedom that Christ has set us free. Stand firm, then, and do not let yourselves be burdened again by a yoke of slavery" **(Galatians 5:1).**

Pause & Reflect

Take a look at the final Quote for the Day. Which of these identity hijackers are you most vulnerable to? Do you recognize yourself in any of them? Or is there another one you can think of that hasn't been included in the list above?

....

....

....

A PRAYER FOR TODAY

God, you made me and know me. You know who I really am. When my identity has been subverted, misdirected, and hijacked, please restore me to my true self. Please restore me to my true calling. And please restore me to you.

In Jesus's name,

Amen

Day 1 Identity Hijacked

Today's Topic
THE ROARING LION AND THE GOOD SHEPHERD

"Be alert and of sober mind. Your enemy the devil prowls around like a roaring lion looking for someone to devour. Resist him, standing firm in the faith, because you know that the family of believers throughout the world is undergoing the same kind of sufferings." (1 Peter 5:8–9)

The Bible is not quiet on this issue: There is an adversary who is seeking to hijack your identity, your life, and your soul. He is seeking not just to tempt and distract you from your true purpose, but ultimately to devour you completely. He intends to "steal and kill and destroy" as Jesus tells us openly in John 10:10, but "I have come that they may have life, and have it to the full."

This is real stalking, predatory behavior. It's dark, it's sinister, and it is targeting you. Is this true? Yes. Should it scare us? No. The Bible is open about these looming attacks precisely so that we will be prepared and won't be caught unawares. By knowing whom we're fighting and which battle we're in, we can put on the armor of God (Ephesians 6) and train for victory in battle. Like a good Father, God doesn't want us to be ignorant of the real threat; he doesn't want us to—lacking prior intelligence—be surprised and overcome.

We are, after all, conquerors. We do, after all, belong to the risen Christ, the one who overcame sin, death, and the grave. Satan is no threat to him at all. He has already been cast down, overcome, and put in his place. His days are numbered, his power is limited, and he is truly defeated.

Nonetheless, he can cause terrible tragedy and suffering in our lives. At times we will be wounded in battle and that is when we will have to retreat to some quiet waters so our souls can be refreshed, our wounds can be tended to, and we can be reminded of God's loving provision, protection, and care.

When our identities are hijacked, be it from attacks from the outside or confusion, doubt, and discouragement within, what we need to do is *remember*. The people of Israel needed reminders of who they were and Whose they were all the time. How many times did God tell his people to build an altar of remembrance? How many religious festivals did he set in place to help them remember God's goodness and grace (even deliverance!) toward them? Why were they supposed to place Scripture on their doorstep? Why do orthodox Jews wear fragments of Scripture on their arms and foreheads, even to this day? To help them remember.

We are no different. We are just as forgetful of God's goodness and grace toward us. The lessons we learn are short-lived and our transformation process is slow. How many times have you had to learn the same lesson over and over? Yeah, same here. Like sheep, we are weak and prone to wander but thankfully we are in the loving care of a good shepherd. (John 10:14) When we stray, He will go after us. When we're lost, He will come find us. And when we err, He will teach us and lead us back home to our flock, where we belong.

Look Inside

Has your identity ever been hijacked? By whom or what?

How often would you say your identity is hijacked in a typical day? Which of these options best describes you?

- ✝ Yes, it is all the time.
- ✝ Not very often; I feel like my identity is pretty stable and I am able to ward off hijackers regularly.
- ✝ Yes, regularly, but things are getting more stable.
- ✝ I have experienced one big hijacking in my life.
- ✝ I deal with lots of small, constant distractions that throw me off my game.
- ✝ I am not aware of having been hijacked but now that I've read this chapter, I am not so sure.
- ✝ I know I've been hijacked but I'm not so sure I've ever been restored.

What stirs in your heart as you read the following quote from p. 69 of the *Emotional Intelligence Christ* Book: "The woman at the well thought that she *was* her struggle and Jesus restored who she really was: a child of God who encountered her Savior."

Have you ever identified with a struggle of yours so much that you believed you *were* your struggle? Have you been able to sort out the difference between your struggle and your true self? If so, who or what helped you recognize the difference? How did that realization come about?

_____
_____
_____
_____
_____

To Sum It Up

- ✞ The devil is a roaring lion, seeking to devour us but our victory in Christ is secure.
- ✞ Jesus is a good shepherd, who tends to his flock and goes after the sheep that go astray.
- ✞ Remembering who God is and who He has been for us can help preserve and restore our identity in Him.
- ✞ Knowing God's word can help us fend off the temptations of passion, popularity, possessions, and power, as Jesus did.

Meditation Moment

Meditate on the passage below and prayerfully put on the full armor of God. Ask God to equip you for every good work ahead and to help you fend off the fiery darts of the evil one.

> Finally, be strong in the Lord and in his mighty power. Put on the full armor of God, so that you can take your stand against the devil's schemes. For our struggle is not against flesh and blood, but against the rulers, against the authorities, against the powers of this dark world and against the spiritual forces of evil in the heavenly realms. Therefore, put on the full armor of God, so that when the day of evil comes, you may be able to stand your ground, and after you have done everything, to stand. Stand firm then, with the belt of truth buckled around your waist, with the breastplate of righteousness in place, and with your feet fitted with the readiness that comes from the gospel of peace. In addition to all this, take up the shield of faith, with which you can extinguish all the flaming arrows of the evil one. Take the helmet of salvation and the sword of the Spirit, which is the word of God. (Ephesians 6:10–17)

Action Items

✝ Read this week's memory verse (along with the reference where it can be found) three times and manually write it out here:

_____

_____

_____

✝ The only way to know you're being hijacked is to be clear on who you truly are. Review your notes from the previous week and remind yourself of your true identity in Christ.

✝ Don't be caught unawares. Make yourself an action plan. What will you do the next time you're tempted by passion (as described in the opening quote)? How will you counter it? How will you practice self-control in that moment? The next time you struggle with jealousy, how can you counter that with generosity? How can you counter the need for recognition and popularity with authenticity? And how can you respond to the temptation of power with humility?

✝ Choose one temptation that tends to hijack your identity and commit to living into its opposite (your true self) today.

EIC = ENCOUNTER + IDENTIFIED BEHAVIOR + COURSE CORRECT

DAILY EIC REFLECTION

ENCOUNTER (E)

Describe one Christ Encounter you had today on the lines below. What happened? Where were you? Whom did you encounter? If you're not sure which one to choose, ask the Holy Spirit to highlight one God-ordained Encounter for you.

_____

_____

_____

_____

_____

IDENTIFIED BEHAVIOR (I)

What behaviors did you act out? Drawing on your newfound understanding in today's lesson, which of your own personality traits and motivations were at play? What were the other person's personality traits and motivations that influenced the encounter? Describe them here:

My unique personality traits and motivations:

The other person's unique personality traits and motivations:

How did these distinct traits and motivations interact with each other? Was there a clash? Did they complement each other? Reflect on this below:

COURSE CORRECT (C)

How did you respond? On a Spirit scale from 1–10, how did you do? Were you able to thoughtfully respond rather than react? Did you successfully surrender to God's will and course correct before you took action? Is there anything you wish you had done differently? Remember that we are going for *progress over perfection*. We are all here to learn and grow. Which lessons would you like to take with you going forward? What did you learn? Reflect on your answers to these questions below:

| 1 | 2 | 3 | 4 | 5 | 6 | 7 | 8 | 9 | 10 |

_____
_____
_____
_____
_____
_____
_____
_____

Quote for the Day

"You have the DNA of God as you are created in the image and likeness of God. You have the ability to soar through the storms of life, all things are possible for you when it comes to mastering your mind for transformation and revival in, through, and with Jesus. Jesus meets you and escorts you back into a personal identity revival." (EIC, p. 50)

"Jesus is all about identity recovery." (EIC, p. 51)

Day 2
IDENTITY RESTORED

What God's Word Says

"So then, just as you received Christ Jesus as Lord, continue to live your lives in him, rooted and built up in him, strengthened in the faith as you were taught, and overflowing with thankfulness. See to it that no one takes you captive through hollow and deceptive philosophy, which depends on human tradition and the elemental spiritual forces of this world rather than on Christ. For in Christ all the fullness of the Deity lives in bodily form, and in Christ you have been brought to fullness" **(Colossians 2:6–10)**.

Pause & Reflect

Are you aware of any parts of your identity that have been hijacked and need to be recovered? Which parts of your true self do you think you have lost along the way?

....
....
....
....
....
....
....
....
....

A PRAYER FOR TODAY

Lord God, you made me and know my true identity. You also know the things that have distorted it. My choices, the choices of others, my responses to the choices of others . . . there is so much that has been broken and seemingly lost. Would you please restore my true identity?

I ask that anything that has been stolen would be restored, anything that has been broken would be mended, and anything that has been distorted or twisted would be made right. Fill in the gaps where something is missing. Complete your work in me. "Restore to me the joy of your salvation" (Psalm 51:12) and the joy of being my whole, restored self.

In Jesus's name,

Amen

Today's Topic
YOU BRING RESTORATION

When we think about the grand theme of Scripture, the sweeping narrative of God's word, we can readily admit that it's ultimately all about God restoring all things to their rightful place. Many theologians have summarized the progression of salvation history in the following terms: Creation–Fall–Redemption–Restoration. Restoration is our ultimate end, both collectively and individually. Restoration is the reason Jesus came into the world, restoration is why God makes his appeal to us through Christ, and restoration is also why God makes his appeal to the world through us. He loves seeing broken hearts mended, broken relationships restored, and wounded communities healed.

And since the birth of Christianity, Christians have found ways to be part of this narrative as well. Whether God's love has compelled them to start orphanages, educate children, house the homeless, rehome refugees, or care for the sick and dying, it is the heart of God for our world that has compelled innumerable acts of sacrificial love.

It's funny how it works: God's love heals the world. But it is the church, God's hands and feet in the world, that is tasked with letting the world know, experience, and feel this love. How better to reach the world than to love it? The love of God compels us, transforms us, and changes how we see people:

> So from now on we regard no one from a worldly point of view. Though we once regarded Christ in this way, we do so no longer. Therefore, if anyone is in Christ, the new creation has come: The old has gone, the new is here! All this is from God, who reconciled us to himself through Christ and gave us the ministry of reconciliation: that God was reconciling the world to himself in Christ, not counting people's sins against them. And he has committed to us the message of reconciliation. We are therefore Christ's ambassadors, as though God were making his appeal through us. We implore you on Christ's behalf: Be reconciled to God. (2 Corinthians 5:16–20)

Reconciliation and restoration are recurring themes throughout Scripture. Take, for example, the story of Joseph, who was ultimately reconciled to the very same brothers who had previously tried to kill him. Take the story of Moses, interceding on behalf of his people before God. Take the story of Abraham, interceding for Sodom and Gomorrah, negotiating with God on their behalf. And finally take Jesus, dying on the cross to reconcile us to our Creator while asking God to forgive those who were torturing him.

Reconciliation is costly. Reconciliation is precious and it comes at a price. But in a way it is also simple. Sometimes all it takes is a glance, a smile, a recognition of wrong, a simple apology. When you think of the man dying beside Jesus on the cross, setting his fellow thief straight and acknowledging that Jesus did not deserve to be there, the response he receives is: "Truly I tell you, today you will be with me in paradise." (Luke 23:43) And all it took was a sincere acknowledgment of his own sin and a true recognition of who Jesus is. That right there was enough to reconcile him to the God who makes all things new.

Look Inside

What do Jesus's words, "I am making all things new" (Revelation 21:5) mean to you personally?

_____
_____
_____
_____

Do you believe he is capable of restoring all things?
- ☦ Yes, I am counting on it!
- ☦ Yeah, but it's kind of hard to wrap my mind around.
- ☦ I'm not sure I know what that means.
- ☦ No. There is no way anyone could do that.

Of the four "shiny objects" listed on EIC p. 51, which one do you think tempts you the most?
- ☦ power
- ☦ popularity
- ☦ passion
- ☦ position

Recall a time when one of these items hijacked your identity. How did it happen? What do you think made you vulnerable to being hijacked?

_____
_____
_____
_____

Do you believe a simple apology is all it takes to be restored? Why or why not?

To Sum It Up

- ✞ God's love changes how we see ourselves and other people.
- ✞ Because God is our Creator, He also has the power to re-create, restore, and heal us.
- ✞ The ultimate outcome of salvation history is restoration.
- ✞ Sometimes all it takes to be reconciled to God is a simple confession of our sin and acknowledgment of who he is.

Meditation Moment

Meditate on this passage from Revelation 21:5: "He who was seated on the throne said, 'I am making everything new!' Then he said, 'Write this down, for these words are trustworthy and true.'"

Our Creator God, who created all things in the first place, also has the power to re-create, restore, renew, reconcile, rebuild, and heal. Allow your heart and your mind to ponder this for a while. What might he currently be restoring in your life?

Action Items

- ✞ Read this week's memory verse out loud three times, each time trying to commit more of it to memory. Think about what it means and why each of the words were chosen when it was originally written. Create any memory aids you can think of. Rather than read it in print, read your own handwritten version (from yesterday) to help you memorize it.
- ✞ Which ministries in your area are participating in the renewing and restoring work of God in the world? Consider getting involved.
- ✞ Thank God for the way he is restoring your true identity in Him.
- ✞ Listen to "Restoration" by David Brymer on YouTube.
- ✞ Thank God for everything He is restoring to you today.

EIC = ENCOUNTER + IDENTIFIED BEHAVIOR + COURSE CORRECT

Daily EIC Reflection

ENCOUNTER (E)

Describe one Christ Encounter you had today on the lines below. What happened? Where were you? Whom did you encounter? If you're not sure which one to choose, ask the Holy Spirit to highlight one God-ordained Encounter for you.

_____
_____
_____
_____

IDENTIFIED BEHAVIOR (I)

What behaviors did you act out? Drawing on your newfound understanding in today's lesson, which of your own personality traits and motivations were at play? What were the other person's personality traits and motivations that influenced the encounter? Describe them here:

My unique personality traits and motivations:

_____
_____
_____
_____

The other person's unique personality traits and motivations:

_____
_____
_____
_____
_____
_____

How did these distinct traits and motivations interact with each other? Was there a clash? Did they complement each other? Reflect on this below:

COURSE CORRECT (C)

How did you respond? On a Spirit scale from 1–10, how did you do? Were you able to thoughtfully respond rather than react? Did you successfully surrender to God's will and course correct before you took action? Is there anything you wish you had done differently? Remember that we are going for *progress over perfection*. We are all here to learn and grow. Which lessons would you like to take with you going forward? What did you learn? Reflect on your answers to these questions below:

Quote for the Day

"Jesus modeled for you true inner freedom, as He was not confined by status or the opinions of other people. When He walked on earth, He had one source of authority in his life: His Father, our Father." (EIC, p. 49)

"Later in Peter's ministry, Peter experienced a physical jailbreak (Acts 12:3–11) when an angel of the Lord entered his prison cell, released the chains that bound him, and walked him out of prison." (EIC, p. 78)

Day 3
JESUS'S AUTHORITY TO SET US FREE

What God's Word Says

"He went to Nazareth, where he had been brought up, and on the Sabbath day he went into the synagogue, as was his custom. He stood up to read, and the scroll of the prophet Isaiah was handed to him. Unrolling it, he found the place where it is written:

> 'The Spirit of the Lord is on me,
>> because he has anointed me
>> to proclaim good news to the poor.
>
> He has sent me to proclaim freedom for the prisoners
>> and recovery of sight for the blind,
>
> to set the oppressed free,
>> to proclaim the year of the Lord's favor.'

"Then he rolled up the scroll, gave it back to the attendant and sat down. The eyes of everyone in the synagogue were fastened on him. He began by saying to them, 'Today this scripture is fulfilled in your hearing'" **(Luke 4:16–20).**

"'Be quiet!' Jesus said sternly. 'Come out of him!' Then the demon threw the man down before them all and came out without injuring him. All the people were amazed and said to each other, 'What words these are! With authority and power he gives orders to impure spirits and they come out!' And the news about him spread throughout the surrounding area" **(Luke 4:35–36).**

Pause & Reflect

Does Jesus have the power to set you free from any and all bondage? If so, why? If not, why not?

_____
_____
_____
_____
_____
_____
_____
_____
_____
_____

A PRAYER FOR TODAY

Jesus, I praise you and worship you! All authority in heaven and on earth has been given to you. You have the power to set the captives free, give sight to the blind, make the lame walk, release the oppressed, and free us from every kind of bondage. Nothing is too big for you, none of your children are too lost or confused, none of our sins are too big for you to forgive. If you speak the word, we will be healed. If you are willing, we will be made clean. And if you decide to deliver us, we will be delivered. Thank you from the bottom of my heart that you choose to use your power for our benefit. You are amazing!

In Jesus's name,

Amen

Day 3 Jesus's Authority to Set Us Free

Today's Topic
JAILBREAK!

Chains broken. Gates opened. Earth shaken. Guards stymied.

Weren't they just here?

The empty grave. The stone rolled away. The seal broken.

Where did he go?

The blind seeing. The deaf hearing. The lame jumping.

What is happening?

The troubled rejoicing. The shy proclaiming. The uneducated preaching.

Who IS this God?

He's a wonder. Come and see!

Look Inside

Do you really believe that Jesus has all of the authority and power the Bible claims He does? If so, how deeply do you think you have internalized this conviction?

- ✟ Yes, Jesus has all authority in heaven and on earth. If I didn't believe that, I wouldn't be here today.
- ✟ I know this is true in my head, but I don't think I can really grasp what this means.
- ✟ There have been times in my life when I have been really in touch with this, but I feel out of touch with Christ's power right now.
- ✟ I am not really sure I believe this. After all, He was just another human.
- ✟ No, I don't.

Have you ever been to an event where "all the people were amazed"? What was it? A concert? A sporting event? Something else?

What made it so amazing?

What amazes you about Jesus?

_____
_____
_____
_____

Has Jesus delivered you from any kind of bondage, slavery, limitation, or confinement? What happened? How did it come about? Write it down, then tell at least one friend this story.

_____
_____
_____
_____
_____
_____
_____
_____
_____

To Sum It Up

- ☦ All authority in heaven and on earth has been given to Jesus.
- ☦ When the people saw his authority and power, they were amazed.
- ☦ Whether you're confined by an internal "jail" or by external circumstances, Jesus can set you free.
- ☦ Jesus models a life of true inner freedom for us.

Meditation Moment

Imagine you are Peter, sitting with Silas in a jail cell. You've been singing for a few hours now, and a supernatural joy has overcome you. Your circumstances aren't looking too promising, but somehow this joy is greater. God's presence is tangible and your confidence in Him hasn't left you; Silas' presence and encouragement is a great help too.

Suddenly something happens! There is loud clanging and shaking and for a moment you're disoriented. What just happened? You look at each other and look around: What? The chains—where did they go? A tremendous sense of exuberant relief and praise overcome you. What an amazing miracle! What a good God! We are set free!

(Of course this is not the end of the story. For the rest of the story, read Acts 12.)

Action Items

- ✞ Record this week's memory verse on your phone (any voice recording app will do) in your own voice and listen to it three times throughout your day. Speak slowly as you record. As you listen to the recording, try following along with your own recorded voice.
- ✞ In your journal this week, keep a running list of things that amaze you about Jesus. Every time something strikes you as amazing, add it to the list and see how many you can collect this week.
- ✞ The next time you realize you are being limited, oppressed, or confined by something or someone, stop for a minute and remember Paul and Silas in prison. Then ask God to set you free as well.
- ✞ Are there any ministries in your community that focus on healing and deliverance? How about freedom from human trafficking and modern-day slavery? Consider calling them and getting involved.
- ✞ Thank God for setting you free from the power of sin and death!

EIC = ENCOUNTER + IDENTIFIED BEHAVIOR + COURSE CORRECT

Daily EIC Reflection

ENCOUNTER (E)

Describe one Christ Encounter you had today on the lines below. What happened? Where were you? Whom did you encounter? If you're not sure which one to choose, ask the Holy Spirit to highlight one God-ordained Encounter for you.

IDENTIFIED BEHAVIOR (I)

What behaviors did you act out? Drawing on your newfound understanding in today's lesson, which of your own personality traits and motivations were at play? What were the other person's personality traits and motivations that influenced the encounter? Describe them here:

My unique personality traits and motivations:

The other person's unique personality traits and motivations:

How did these distinct traits and motivations interact with each other? Was there a clash? Did they complement each other? Reflect on this below:

COURSE CORRECT (C)

How did you respond? On a Spirit scale from 1–10, how did you do? Were you able to thoughtfully respond rather than react? Did you successfully surrender to God's will and course correct before you took action? Is there anything you wish you had done differently? Remember that we are going for *progress over perfection*. We are all here to learn and grow. Which lessons would you like to take with you going forward? What did you learn? Reflect on your answers to these questions below:

FLESH					SP	SPI	SPIR	SPIRIT	SPIRIT	SPIRIT
1	2	3	4	5	6	7	8	9	10

_____
_____
_____
_____
_____
_____
_____
_____
_____

QUOTE FOR THE DAY

"Jesus' invitation to all of us began with his command to Thomas in John 20:27, 'Stop doubting and believe.' Give more authority to the strength of God's Holy Spirit within you than to your circumstance." (EIC, p. 58)

"As we encounter Christ in humble truth and honesty as the woman at the well did, we too resurrect confidence and love within our identity which gives us power and authority over our mind, will, and emotions." (EIC, p. 67)

"Think about letting go of all that you are into the hands and heart of Jesus Christ—a complete surrender and leaning into Jesus. Similar to letting go of a stone into a calm body of water and observing the ripple effect, the act of letting go of YOU into HIM results in a ripple effect of positivity that cascades through your identity, beliefs, capabilities, behavior, and environment." (EIC, p. 72)

Day 4
CHOOSING FREEDOM

What God's Word Says

"'What do you want me to do for you?' Jesus asked him. The blind man said, 'Rabbi I want to see.' 'Go,' said Jesus, 'your faith has healed you.' Immediately he received his sight and followed Jesus along the road." **(Mark 10:51–52)**.

"Ask and it will be given to you; seek and you will find; knock and the door will be opened to you. For everyone who asks receives; the one who seeks finds; and to the one who knocks, the door will be opened" **(Matthew 7:7–8)**.

Pause & Reflect

What are you doing to actively participate in becoming spiritually healed and set free? How are you knocking, asking, and seeking at the moment?

....

....

....

A Prayer for Today

God, you have all the power. But somehow—miraculously, mysteriously—you want me to partner with you for my healing. You want me to show up, you want me to be engaged, you want me to *want* to be made whole. Some days I don't even see the need for your healing touch or your word of deliverance. When I don't care, when I am apathetic to my spiritual condition, please nudge me awake again. Make me alert to you and the work you are doing in me. Awaken me to your Spirit. Help me to choose you. Strengthen my resolve to be made whole and encourage me to never stop asking, knocking, and seeking for you.

In Jesus's name,

Amen

Today's Topic
ASK. SEEK. KNOCK.

"Ask and it will be given to you; seek and you will find; knock and the door will be opened to you." (Matthew 7:7) What a bold claim! And it raises the question: How much power do we have, really? Isn't God the one who is all-powerful and aren't we simply supposed to humbly and meekly accept our lot in life? Doesn't being a Christian mean being a passive accepter of the *status quo*? Doesn't it mean simply being kind and praying for our enemies?

Not according to Matthew 7, where we are encouraged to actively engage with God and reach for more. Asking, seeking, and knocking are not for the passive, despondent, disinterested, disillusioned, or checked out. They are acts of stepping out in faith. We only ask, seek, and knock if we believe it can make a difference; we only ask, seek, and knock if we believe God invites and wants our active participation, if we believe he cares enough to listen and engage with us.

When we ask ourselves if God hears, we think of Moses interceding for the people of Israel. Or Abraham interceding for Sodom and Gomorrah. God didn't seem offended by their requests; he engaged them. He didn't seem put off by their audacious statements—instead, he interacted with them. Of course, you might argue that they were special . . . and they were. They walked closely with God and shared a degree of intimacy with Him that most of us can only aspire to. But they weren't perfect. The Bible is refreshingly honest about their shortfalls and failings. It is not a work of propaganda that only highlights the positive aspects of the heroes of the faith; instead it reveals to us the very human, very fallible, very vulnerable and frail nature of the saints who have gone before, made mistakes, and still have been commended for their faith (Hebrews 11).

So, without placing them on so high a pedestal that we don't dare attempt to imitate them, let's allow ourselves to be challenged by their example. Let's learn from them how to walk so closely with God every day that He considers us a close friend. Let's learn to listen before we speak as we pray. Let's nurture our relationship with God by fully showing up for it. One way we know to do that is by trusting and obeying His word. Another is by spending time with Him and serving our neighbor. And yet another is by courageously, honestly, and sincerely engaging with Him by asking, seeking, and knocking in word and deed.

Look Inside

Recall a time in your life when you were actively asking, seeking, and knocking about something. What happened?

When was the last time you showed up for your relationship with God wholeheartedly? Whether you were bringing disappointment, anger, or joy to him, when did you bring a request before Him passionately, openly, and sincerely?

- ✞ It's been a while.
- ✞ Yup, just a few minutes ago!
- ✞ I struggle to keep things real with God.
- ✞ All the time.

Why do you think it is that God wants to engage our wills in our sanctification process? Why doesn't he just heal and restore us completely in every possible way the moment we become Christians? What is the value of contending with him in prayer?

As you reflect on your prayer life, what role does interceding for others play in it? How much of your asking, seeking, and knocking is on behalf of others?

- ✞ Maybe 10%.
- ✞ I'd say 30%. Whenever someone comes to mind.
- ✞ A good 50%. I intercede for others intentionally and regularly.
- ✞ 70%. Praying for others is really important to me.

If the only thing standing between you and your freedom is having enough faith to ask for it, what is it you would like to ask for right now?

To Sum It Up

- ✝ In Christ, we have power and authority over our mind, will, and emotions.
- ✝ God wants to partner with us in our sanctification process.
- ✝ Showing up for our relationship with God wholeheartedly matters.
- ✝ We worship a God who encourages us to engage with him by asking, seeking, and knocking.

Meditation Moment

Imagine God waiting to give you the most amazing gift of your life and just waiting for you to be ready enough to believe for, ask for, and receive it. Imagine him asking you, "What do you want me to do for you?" Are you ready? Tell him what you want.

Action Items

- ✝ Listen to your recording of this week's Bible verse again. Now try reciting it from memory (without the recording). Can you do it? Don't forget to quote the reference. Keep practicing it until you feel confident.
- ✝ Commit to increasing your intercession time in prayer by at least 10 minutes. Ask God what or who he wants you to be interceding for during that time. Then commit to interceding for that cause or person every day until the issue is resolved.

continued...

Action Items (cont.)

✝ Pick one area of your life you have become despondent or disillusioned about and ask God to give you the faith to keep believing for breakthrough in this area.

✝ Do you want to be set free? What is holding you back? Are you holding on to an old version of yourself that will not allow you to grow? As you identify what is holding you back, select something you find in nature (a stone, a twig, a leaf), take it to a stream, a river, a lake, an ocean, or a pond, and release it, symbolizing an act of your will—your decision to "let go of YOU ino HIM."

EIC = ENCOUNTER + IDENTIFIED BEHAVIOR + COURSE CORRECT

Daily EIC Reflection

ENCOUNTER (E)

Describe one Christ Encounter you had today on the lines below. What happened? Where were you? Whom did you encounter? If you're not sure which one to choose, ask the Holy Spirit to highlight one God-ordained Encounter for you.

IDENTIFIED BEHAVIOR (I)

What behaviors did you act out? Drawing on your newfound understanding in today's lesson, which of your own personality traits and motivations were at play? What were the other person's personality traits and motivations that influenced the encounter? Describe them here:

My unique personality traits and motivations:

....
....
....
....
....
....
....
....
....
....

The other person's unique personality traits and motivations:

....
....
....
....
....
....
....
....
....
....

How did these distinct traits and motivations interact with each other? Was there a clash? Did they complement each other? Reflect on this below:

....
....
....

Day 4 Choosing Freedom

_____
_____
_____
_____
_____
_____
_____
_____

COURSE CORRECT (C)

How did you respond? On a Spirit scale from 1–10, how did you do? Were you able to thoughtfully respond rather than react? Did you successfully surrender to God's will and course correct before you took action? Is there anything you wish you had done differently? Remember that we are going for *progress over perfection*. We are all here to learn and grow. Which lessons would you like to take with you going forward? What did you learn? Reflect on your answers to these questions below:

1   2   3   4   5   6   7   8   9   10

_____
_____
_____
_____
_____
_____
_____
_____

QUOTE FOR THE DAY

"Lean into the Lover of your soul and allow Him to replace any misplaced desire with an undivided heart that seeks His kingship and authority within your heart, mind, will, and emotions." (EIC, p. 60)

Day 5

AN UNDIVIDED HEART

What God's Word Says

> Teach me your way, Lord,
>   that I may rely on your faithfulness;
> give me an undivided heart,
>   that I may fear your name.
> I will praise you, Lord my God, with all my heart;
>   I will glorify your name forever" **(Psalm 86:11–12)**.

"I will give them an undivided heart and put a new spirit in them; I will remove from them their heart of stone and give them a heart of flesh. Then they will follow my decrees and be careful to keep my laws. They will be my people, and I will be their God" **(Ezekiel 11:19–20)**.

Pause & Reflect

Why do you think God cares so much about our hearts being undivided? What do you think we lose out on when they are not?

_____
_____
_____
_____
_____
_____
_____

Day 5 An Undivided Heart

A PRAYER FOR TODAY

God, I am aware that I hold back. My trust in you is limited and I have a hard time fully believing that you are good. I also admit that everything I do is piecemeal. Nothing I do is completely wholehearted; I rarely give anything 100%. And yet you ask for my whole heart. You want me to love you with abandon. You want me to show up to my life and to you and my neighbor wholeheartedly. Even if my heart's been broken, even if I've been disappointed or hurt, you want me to heal and receive your love so I can love as you do.

Please heal my heart. I want to be a wholehearted person. I want my heart to be undivided. I want to be able to commit. I don't want to be "like a wave of the sea, blown and tossed by the wind" (James 1:6) "double-minded and unstable in all [I] do." (James 1:8) Instead, I want to be more like you—clear on my identity, clear on my calling, clear on my vision and purpose, and joyfully clear on who you are for me. Please give me an undivided heart and put a new spirit in me.

In Jesus's name,

Amen

Today's Topic
THE BEAUTY OF AN UNDIVIDED HEART

Consider the following scenes:

1. Two young women are sitting across from each other at the restaurant. One of them leaning in, animatedly telling her story—her eyes wide, her hands expressive—the other leaning back in her chair, alternatingly staring blankly out the window and then scrolling on her phone.
2. An elderly couple is sitting on a park bench, watching the sunset together. Their things (purses, grocery bags, electronics) are set aside and they are quietly taking in the view and sharing in the experience. Occasionally they exchange words, but mostly they sit in silence.
3. The doctor enters the scared patient's room and never looks up from her chart. The patient is fidgeting with his hands, nervous and overwhelmed by the diagnosis, a barrage of questions filling his mind. But the doctor never makes eye contact with the patient, only asks yes/no questions, and abruptly leaves the room when her allotted time is over, leaving no time for the patient to ask questions or express his concerns.

How present were each of these people to each other? How distracted or divided were they? How precious would undivided attention have been to the woman telling her story or the man trying to grapple with his diagnosis? How valuable, transformative, nurturing, and even healing could it have been?

We have forgotten the value of slowing down, listening well, and being present to each other. For decades now we have been trying to be everywhere but here. We are so caught up with doing everything simultaneously that we no longer know how to do one thing well. And so, we see children at the playground getting into fights while their parents are engrossed in social media on their phones. We miss what is important because we are preoccupied with being occupied.

When God says he will give the Israelites an undivided heart, he is also saying he wants to take away their heart of stone and give them a heart of flesh. He wants us to see the humanity in people and situations. Not just be logical and exact and efficient all the time. He wants us to have tender hearts of flesh.

Being undivided wouldn't automatically have to mean that, would it? It could mean lazor-sharp "don't interrupt me now" focus until a task is done. But that is not the undivided heart God is referring to here. Instead, this heart is focusing on something with undivided attention that makes it softer, more human, of flesh: our loving Creator God. If we give him our undivided focus and attention, he will soften our hearts. He will transform us and make us new, put a new spirit in us. By making room for God, we suddenly have room for others. By receiving God's love, we suddenly have abundance from which to give.

Becoming undivided is not a one-time task we complete once and must never address again. It is something we must constantly recommit to. It's a matter of getting our priorities straight, aligned with God's priorities, despite the fact that there are so many distractions clamoring for our attention. In fact, people spend big money on distracting us! In many ways, our time and attention are the only currency we have. Let's spend it wisely and, like Saint Augustine, ask God to "order our loves."[1] Only when God orders our priorities and our undivided hearts are set on Him will we be spending our lives on the right things, following God's call, and fulfilling our purpose.

Look Inside

On a scale from 1 to 10, how distractable are you?

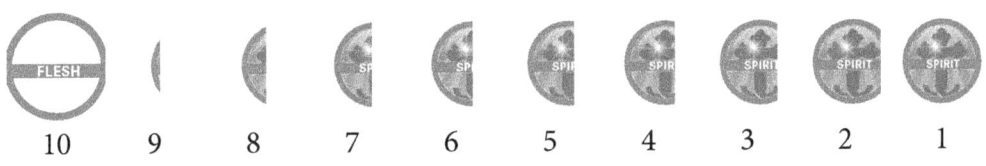

Is there anything or anyone you can give your undivided attention to for hours on end? What is it? What is it about that thing or that person that draws you in and holds your attention?

....
....
....
....

Which of these experiences would you prefer:

1. 3 hours with someone who is distracted, irritable, and emotionally unavailable.
2. 1 hour with someone you admire. They won't be talking to you; they will be near you and you get to watch them, but they will be interacting with someone else.
3. 10 minutes with someone who sees you, knows you, hears you, and gives you their full attention.

What would you give or how much would you pay for one hour of your personal hero's undivided attention?

How much of your heart do you think God has today?
- ✝ At the moment I think God has less than 20% of my heart.
- ✝ I give him about 30%. He has occasional access to my heart and sometimes I listen to him. Other times I choose to ignore him.
- ✝ I think he has about 70% of my heart. I try to make Him a priority and give things over to Him in trust and love. But I still doubt and fear regularly and get carried away by my own desires.
- ✝ God's got my whole heart. He rules and reigns over my decisions and has the director's chair in my life. I am not perfect, but I am completely dedicated to loving God and growing in that love every day.

Finish this sentence: When my heart is undivided, I am . . .

To Sum It Up
- ✝ Allow God to replace any misplaced desire with an undivided heart.
- ✝ We miss what is important because we are preoccupied with being occupied.
- ✝ If we give God our undivided focus and attention, he will soften our hearts.
- ✝ Only when God orders our priorities and our undivided hearts are set on Him will we be spending our lives on the right things, following God's call, and fulfilling our purpose.

Day 5 An Undivided Heart

MEDITATION MOMENT

Pray an adaptation of Ezekiel 11:19–20, asking God to give you an undivided heart:

God, please give me an undivided heart and put a new spirit in me; please remove my heart of stone and give me a heart of flesh. Then I will follow your decrees and be careful to keep your laws. I will belong to you, and you will be my God.

In Jesus's name,

Amen

Action Items

- ✝ Write this week's Bible verse out from memory on the lines below. Don't cheat! Once you have written it out and reviewed it, go back and check it with your handwritten original. How did you do?

_____

_____

_____

- ✝ The next time you realize you are frazzled because you are preoccupied with being occupied, schedule a 15-minute break in your day to give God your undivided attention. Turn all of your devices off and be present to only Him.
- ✝ Do less. If you're going to give people and things your undivided attention, chances are you won't be able to do as many things as you are right now. Enjoy doing fewer things better.
- ✝ Pray for someone you know whose heart is divided or torn. Ask God to give them peace.

EIC = ENCOUNTER + IDENTIFIED BEHAVIOR + COURSE CORRECT

Daily EIC Reflection

ENCOUNTER (E)

Describe one Christ Encounter you had today on the lines below. What happened? Where were you? Whom did you encounter? If you're not sure which one to choose, ask the Holy Spirit to highlight one God-ordained Encounter for you.

_____
_____
_____
_____
_____

IDENTIFIED BEHAVIOR (I)

What behaviors did you act out? Drawing on your newfound understanding in today's lesson, which of your own personality traits and motivations were at play? What were the other person's personality traits and motivations that influenced the encounter? Describe them here:

My unique personality traits and motivations:

_____
_____
_____
_____

The other person's unique personality traits and motivations:

_____
_____
_____
_____

How did these distinct traits and motivations interact with each other? Was there a clash? Did they complement each other? Reflect on this below:

COURSE CORRECT (C)

How did you respond? On a Spirit scale from 1–10, how did you do? Were you able to thoughtfully respond rather than react? Did you successfully surrender to God's will and course correct before you took action? Is there anything you wish you had done differently? Remember that we are going for *progress over perfection*. We are all here to learn and grow. Which lessons would you like to take with you going forward? What did you learn? Reflect on your answers to these questions below:

Endnotes

1   Saint Augustine is known for the Latin phrase ordo amoris, order our loves. His work has been translated and edited many times. For example: Augustine of Hippo, Late Have I Loved Thee: Selected Writings of Saint Augustine on Love (New York: Vintage Books, 2006).

Intro to Week 3
Self-Control
(Self-Management)

MEMORY VERSE FOR THE WEEK

"Remain in me, as I also remain in you. No branch can bear fruit by itself; it must remain in the vine. Neither can you bear fruit unless you remain in me. I am the vine; you are the branches. If you remain in me and I in you, you will bear much fruit; apart from me you can do nothing" (John 15:4–5).

A SUPPORT RESOURCE FOR THE WEEK TO EXPLORE:

Edge God In Podcast: Connecting To Emotional Intelligence in Christ Step 2 Self-Management/Self-Control
https://edgegodin.com/connecting-emotional-intelligence-in-christ-to-disc-step-2-self-management-self-control/

Welcome Message:

Welcome to Week 3, where we will explore the power of emotional intelligence, self-control, and consistency!

As you know, developing our emotional intelligence in Christ is one of the primary goals of this study. This week we will investigate what self-control has to do with emotional intelligence and why it's so important, work on developing our emotional intelligence overall, and reflect on the value of consistency. Then we will ponder Jesus's question to Peter: "Do you love me?" and consider what it might mean for us too. Finally, we will dwell on the skill and practice of abiding in God's unconditional love.

As we've said before, please engage this process as deeply as possible. Just like any program or tool, you get out of it what you put into it. Allow yourself to be challenged by the questions and reflection opportunities contained here. Allow yourself to be stretched and grow. Enjoy this opportunity to intentionally set aside time for spiritual renewal.

We hope this week's study will encourage you to increase your emotional intelligence, love God more, and abide in His love.

Connecting Hearts in Him,

Estella, Lauren, and Rich

SELF-CONTROL (SELF-MANAGEMENT) WEEK 3

Quote for the Day

"Self-control is the last fruit of the Spirit that resurrects the other fruits to the frontlines of our behaviors. Self-control is the ramification of surrender to the presence and authority of Jesus Christ." (EIC, p. 82)

"So, self-control is a supernatural mastery over the mind, emotions, and will that comes as a result of being transformed by the Spirit of the One who mastered every thought, feeling, and behavior perfectly." (EIC, p. 87)

Day 1
WHAT IS SELF-CONTROL?

What God's Word Says

"But the fruit of the Spirit is love, joy, peace, forbearance, kindness, goodness, faithfulness, gentleness and self-control. Against such things there is no law. Those who belong to Christ Jesus have crucified the flesh with its passions and desires. Since we live by the Spirit, let us keep in step with the Spirit" **(Galatians 5:22–25)**.

"For this reason I remind you to fan into flame the gift of God, which is in you through the laying on of my hands. For the Spirit God gave us does not make us timid, but gives us power, love and self-discipline" **(2 Timothy 1:6–7)**.

Pause & Reflect

On a scale from 1 to 10, how would you rate your self-control? Victory lies in our ability to allow the Holy Spirit to ignite the fruit of self-control within us. Is there one thing you can think of that triggers you and makes you fly off the handle/lose it? What is that?

Self-Control (Self-Management) Week 3

Day 1 What is Self-Control?

A PRAYER FOR TODAY

God, I admit that I could use some more self-control in _____ area. Because it is a fruit of the Spirit, I can ask you for more of it with confidence. Holy Spirit, please fill me with every one of the fruits of the Spirit, especially self-control. Increase my patience, increase my grace, increase my forbearance, and increase my ability to delay gratification. Mature me, God, in you and give me power to overcome the surge of emotions that too often hijacks my ability to practice self-control.

In Jesus's name,

Amen

Today's Topic
EXPRESS YOUR SELF-(CONTROL)!

In this world we are typically encouraged to be true to ourselves, express ourselves, and live loud and proud. For many people, as long as one is open and honest about how one truly feels, all moral obligations have been met. God's standards aren't considered; it's only important that people be true to themselves.

But that is not what we are taught in the Bible. According to God's word, there are standards that go beyond our own wants and desires—a standard beyond our human selves. And we are commanded to follow it. To do so requires tremendous maturity and self-control. None of us do it perfectly but we can all aspire to grow in it.

Imagine a mom in a supermarket with three young children, all wanting to run in different directions. Overwhelmed, she may want to yell at them but in order not to, she must use self-control. Or a disappointed teenager who lost in a competition. He may want to kick something and cuss at his opponent, but he shows sportsmanship by congratulating his opponent and wishing him all the best—this requires self-mastery or self-control. Finally, picture yourself in a challenging situation that instantly makes your blood boil. Can you recall a time when you were able to steady yourself, breathe, and allow the Holy Spirit to take over so you didn't act on those strong feelings in that moment?

These are all examples of self-control. Surprisingly, the way we learn it is not by focusing more on ourselves. Instead, we learn self-control by surrendering to God. Surrender is one of those words that sounds weak and timid but really requires a lot of power and self-mastery. Only strong people can surrender their wills to God. Only powerful people have mastery over themselves.

We wish our culture acknowledged this kind of power more; but it's not always easy to spot. Instead, we witness it by what we *don't* see. When we don't see lust acting out, when we don't see rage, when we don't see impulsive buying or spending or addictions or . . . that is when self-control is at play. When things go well, self-control has often played a part. When a relationship is successful, when communication goes smoothly, when forgiveness and reconciliation take place, when generosity is lived . . . self-control has often played a part.

It's a beautiful and powerful thing, really.

Self-control is particularly difficult to live when we don't see the end in sight. Delaying gratification is one thing when we know we are only delaying it until tomorrow. It is another entirely when we don't know that the resolution will ever come. As we know, "Hope deferred makes the hea rt sick, but a longing fulfilled is a tree of life." (Proverbs 13:12) It's not easy to wait on God and surrender to Him right in the middle of big emotions and/or desires. But, as it is with anything, with practice and the power of the Holy Spirit, we can improve.

Look Inside

Is practicing self-control easy for you?
- ✞ Oh yes, I'm a natural!
- ✞ Not really.
- ✞ It's pretty tough, to be honest.
- ✞ Impossible!
- ✞ I've worked on it a lot and I am improving.

What are some situations you've been in when you were able to practice excellent self-control? What are some situations you recall where you were not able to manage yourself successfully?

_____
_____
_____
_____
_____

Go back to the one area you reflected on in Pause & Reflect. If you could improve your self-control in that one area of your life, what would the benefits be to you? Name at least 5.

1. _____
2. _____
3. _____
4. _____
5. _____

What would the benefits be to others? Name at least 5.

1. _____
2. _____
3. _____
4. _____
5. _____

Self-Control (Self-Management) Week 3

TO SUM IT UP

- ✞ Self-control is a supernatural mastery over the mind, emotions, and will.
- ✞ We learn self-control by surrendering to God.
- ✞ When things go well, self-control has often played a part.
- ✞ With practice and the help of the Holy Spirit, we can increase our capacity for self-control.

MEDITATION MOMENT

Please pray the following prayer (and feel free to add your own words as well):

Lord, I understand that self-control is an important fruit of the Spirit. In fact, it helps me practice all of the other fruits as well. Please increase my desire and capacity for self-control. Please help me practice it and improve. Please give me patience and grace for this process. I surrender to your presence and authority, knowing that with you I am in good hands. Please take good care of me. If I let go, you'd better catch me!

In Jesus's name,

Amen

Action Items

- ✞ Read this week's memory verse (along with the reference where it can be found) three times and manually write it out here:

  _____
  _____
  _____
  _____

- ✞ Ask the Holy Spirit to show you the consequences of your lack of self-control. In the space below, write down the qualities that result from a lack of self-control. In the column to the right write their opposite.

  continued

Lack of Self-Control Produces:	Self-Control Produces:

✟ Pray and confess your left-column traits to God. Then ask God to replace your left-column traits with the corresponding right-column traits (or any others the Holy Spirit brings to mind).

✟ Complete the sentence below with the right-column traits you listed above and state these sentences confidently out loud.

In Christ, I am _____!

In Christ, I am _____!

In Christ, I am _____!

In Christ, I am _____!

In Christ, I am _____!

✟ Ask God to increase your self-control in the one area you've been reflecting on in the Pause & Reflect and Look Inside sections. Tell at least one trusted friend that you would like prayer for increased self-control in that area and ask them to check in on you once a week for a month to see how that is going. Ask them to pray for you as well. Telling someone and reporting to them regularly will make this a more real, actionable goal for you. Then assess if you would like to continue. Maybe you can provide accountability to them as well.

EIC = ENCOUNTER + IDENTIFIED BEHAVIOR + COURSE CORRECT

Daily EIC Reflection

ENCOUNTER (E)

Describe one Christ Encounter you had today on the lines below. What happened? Where were you? Whom did you encounter? If you're not sure which one to choose, ask the Holy Spirit to highlight one God-ordained Encounter for you.

_____
_____
_____
_____
_____
_____
_____
_____
_____

IDENTIFIED BEHAVIOR (I)

Which behaviors can you identify? Drawing on your newfound understanding in today's lesson, which of your own personality traits and motivations were at play? What were the other person's personality traits and motivations that influenced the encounter? Describe them here:

My unique personality traits and motivations:

_____
_____
_____
_____

The other person's unique personality traits and motivations:

_____
_____

Day 1 What is Self-Control?

How did these distinct traits and motivations interact with each other? Was there a clash? Did they complement each other? Reflect on this below:

COURSE CORRECT (C)

How did you respond? On a scale from 1–10, how did you do? Were you able to thoughtfully respond rather than react? Did you successfully surrender to God's will and course correct before you took action? Is there anything you wish you had done differently? Remember that we are going for *progress over perfection*. We are all here to learn and grow. Which lessons would you like to take with you going forward? What did you learn? Reflect on your answers to these questions below:

1	2	3	4	5	6	7	8	9	10

Quote for the Day

"Without self-control, capturing the ability to walk in emotional intelligence is like trying to catch a trout with your hands in a stream; you may grab it for a split second but then it quickly slips out of your hands. In terms of emotional intelligence, self-control is part of self-management which also includes discipline, how we relate to goals, living by principles and personal values, and the ability to adapt to situations, relationships, and feelings." (EIC, p. 86)

"Your awareness of the presence of Christ within you gives you the ability to be the boss of your emotions rather than allowing them to be the boss of you." (EIC, p. 83)

"Self-management flows from knowing one's identity in Christ so profoundly that the useless trinkets and shiny objects of the world, which once gained free rent between your two ears and spilled out into your behavior, are stopped in their tracks. Self-discipline, trustworthiness, transparency, adaptability, and optimistic character emerges to the front lines of your ability to manage your emotions well. The trinkets of needing to be right, liked, understood, seen, acknowledged, and recognized to feel successful, valued, and enough in this world are replaced with a spirit of power, courage, self-control, and an overall feeling of peace despite external triggers." (EIC, p. 83)

Day 2
DEVELOPING EMOTIONAL INTELLIGENCE

What God's Word Says

"An elder must be blameless, faithful to his wife, a man whose children believe and are not open to the charge of being wild and disobedient. Since an overseer manages God's household, he must be blameless—not overbearing, not quick-tempered, not given to drunkenness, not violent, not pursuing dishonest gain. Rather, he must be hospitable, one who loves what is good, who is self-controlled, upright, holy and disciplined. He must hold firmly to the trustworthy message as it has been taught, so that he can encourage others by sound doctrine and refute those who oppose it" **(Titus 1:6–9).**

Pause & Reflect

How many examples of self-discipline and emotional intelligence can you count in the Scripture passage above?

A PRAYER FOR TODAY

God, I am aware that you want to shape my heart and make me more like you. Jesus, I'm in awe of your emotional intelligence and love for people. You knew just when to speak and just when to be silent. Your union with the Father was and is unbroken; you could and can see as He sees. Lord, please develop such emotional intelligence in me too. Without it I cannot love you, the world, and your people as I should.

In Jesus's name,

Amen

Today's Topic
THE CHARACTER GYM

Have you ever walked into a gym and expected to emerge from it that same day with a totally transformed physique? Have you ever tried one of the instant weight-loss fads to help you get in the shape you'd like to be in overnight? Did it work?

Similarly, in order to grow in emotional intelligence and character, we must practice and discipline ourselves daily. It is our daily habits that make the biggest difference, not the occasional extraordinary experience or practice. Repeatedly Paul uses the image of an athlete to spur us on toward love and good deeds.

Athletes know that their performance depends on committed, ongoing training and practice. No Olympian can succeed or even be included in the competition without rigorous daily discipline which permeates and affects all areas of their lives. Our commitments do that to us; they transform us. Once we have defined and committed to the goal we are headed toward, everything else in our lives has to fall in line.

Look Inside

How often do you work out, play a sport, or go to the gym?
- Every day
- 3 to 5 days a week.
- About once a week.
- Occasionally.
- Whenever I feel like it.
- Never.

And how often would you say you engage in spiritual exercises and disciplines that increase your emotional intelligence, self-discipline, and character?
- Every day
- 3 to 5 days a week.
- About once a week.
- Occasionally.
- Whenever I feel like it.
- Never.

Which of these apply to you? Please check all that apply. Are there any items listed here that you are not currently practicing but would be interested in making part of your daily discipline? Circle all you would be interested in exploring.

- ☐ I attend church faithfully.
- ☐ I am a member of a small group.
- ☐ I pray daily.
- ☐ I study the word of God.
- ☐ I nurture open, honest spiritual relationships.
- ☐ I memorize the word of God.
- ☐ I listen to the word of God.
- ☐ I seek out solitude regularly.
- ☐ I make time for worship and adoration.
- ☐ I meditate on the word of God.
- ☐ I serve the people of God.
- ☐ I serve the least of these.
- ☐ I share God's word with others.
- ☐ I meet with a spiritual director.
- ☐ I have an accountability partner.
- ☐ I journal and reflect on my day daily.
- ☐ I ask myself hard questions and am open to other people challenging me and asking me hard questions.
- ☐ I have a therapist.
- ☐ I invite truth-tellers into my life.
- ☐ I apply Scripture to my daily life.
- ☐ I engage in spiritual reading.
- ☐ I make time to accept and respond to God's unconditional love.
- ☐ I have a mentor.
- ☐ I mentor someone else.

Ask Jesus how He practiced such amazing self-discipline and displayed such amazing emotional intelligence and character so consistently. Write down His response in the lines below (what you imagine He would say).

_____
_____
_____
_____
_____

To Sum It Up

- ✞ Your awareness of the presence of Christ within you gives you the ability to be the boss of your emotions.
- ✞ Self-management flows from knowing one's identity in Christ.
- ✞ The things we're committed to challenge and change us.
- ✞ Jesus is the pioneer and perfecter of our faith.

Day 2 Developing Emotional Intelligence

Meditation Moment

When we go to the gym, we can measure our success/progress by measuring our body weight, heart rate, endurance, flexibility, core strength, and a number of other metrics. But how do we know we are growing in spiritual maturity, fortitude, character, strength, and endurance? How do we know our emotional intelligence in Christ is increasing? Consider which metrics you will be looking for in the future to measure whether you are growing spiritually.

Action Items

✝ Read this week's memory verse out loud three times, each time trying to commit more of it to memory. Think about what it means and why each of the words were chosen when it was originally written. Create any memory aids you can think of. Rather than read it in print, read your own handwritten version (from yesterday) to help you memorize it.

   ✝ The next time you find yourself beating yourself up with negative self-talk, stop yourself and ask God to help you put on His "goggles." How does He see you now, in the midst of your disappointment/anger/disillusion? Ask Him to help you see yourself as He sees you.

   ✝ Commit to adding one new spiritual discipline to your routine this week. Ask the Holy Spirit to assist you in the area of self-control.

   ✝ Select one of the items you circled under Look Inside and commit to practicing it every day this week. Note what you learn. How is this practice changing you? How is it changing your perception of God? Your ability to choose how you spend your time, attention and focus?

EIC = ENCOUNTER + IDENTIFIED BEHAVIOR + COURSE CORRECT

Daily EIC Reflection

ENCOUNTER (E)

Describe one Christ Encounter you had today on the lines below. What happened? Where were you? Whom did you encounter? If you're not sure which one to choose, ask the Holy Spirit to highlight one God-ordained Encounter for you.

....
....
....
....
....
....
....
....

IDENTIFIED BEHAVIOR (I)

Which behaviors can you identify? Drawing on your newfound understanding in today's lesson, which of your own personality traits and motivations were at play? What were the other person's personality traits and motivations that influenced the encounter? Describe them here:

My unique personality traits and motivations:

....
....
....

The other person's unique personality traits and motivations:

....
....

How did these distinct traits and motivations interact with each other? Was there a clash? Did they complement each other? Reflect on this below:

COURSE CORRECT (C)

How did you respond? On a Spirit scale from 1–10, how did you do? Were you able to thoughtfully respond rather than react? Did you successfully surrender to God's will and course correct before you took action? Is there anything you wish you had done differently? Remember that we are going for *progress over perfection*. We are all here to learn and grow. Which lessons would you like to take with you going forward? What did you learn? Reflect on your answers to these questions below:

QUOTE FOR THE DAY

"Self-control allows us to trust God and continue to do good in the midst of undesirable situations." (EIC, p. 88)

"Self-control is the ramification of surrender to the presence and authority of Jesus Christ of Nazareth in your life." (EIC, p. 82)

"The biggest temptation you face in making the journey from discipline to habit will be impatience for measurable and sustainable results." (EIC, p. 94)

Day 3
EMOTIONAL INTELLIGENCE + SELF-CONTROL = CONSISTENCY

What God's Word Says

"Like a city whose walls are broken down is a man who lacks self-control." **(Proverbs 25:28)**

"Better a patient person than a warrior, one with self-control than one who takes a city." **(Proverbs 16:32)**

Pause & Reflect

Would you rather receive a smaller reward now or a larger, more significant reward later?

A PRAYER FOR TODAY

Holy God, you know how much I struggle with patience and self-control. Please give me the grace I need to pause long enough to be able to tune in to your Spirit when I am presented with a challenge. Give me the grace to become more like you.

In Jesus's name,

Amen

Self-Control (Self-Management) Week 3

Today's Topic
THE TORTOISE AND THE HARE

Around the world, US Americans are *not* known for our patience. We are used to immediate service, immediate attention, and immediate solutions. We are not prone to choosing the longer, more arduous (but possibly better) path. We are not naturally inclined to go slow. To many of us, fastest is best.

Have you ever heard of Aesop's famous Fable, *The Tortoise and the Hare*? There are a number of retellings and variations on it, but the gist of it is that the two animals enter a race. The hare is eager and fast and very confident he will win. The tortoise is famous for his inability to move quickly. But this animal is also associated with age and wisdom and because he stays the course and is persistent, he ends up winning the race. Speed, in the end, was not the deciding factor.

In Proverbs 16:32 (see What God's Word Says) a patient person is praised above a mighty warrior and someone with self-control is praised above someone who achieves visible, readily apparent success. This is very different from our culture's value system! Have you ever seen the most patient person in your city paraded through the streets on a national holiday? Have you ever found a listing of top self-controlled people in the Wall Street Journal?

The Bible challenges us to "unplug" from our innate value system and automatic reactions (based on our culture) and "plug in" to the values of the kingdom instead—where the patient are celebrated and the self-controlled are revered.

Look Inside

On a scale from 1 to 10, how self-controlled would you say you are?

Is there anyone in your life whose patience you admire? Who is that? How did you notice they had this quality?

Day 3 Emotional Intelligence + Self-Control = Consistency

How easy is it for you to wait for what you want?
- ✟ I think I'm pretty good at it.
- ✟ So-so.
- ✟ It's tough.
- ✟ It's killing me!

Can you think of a time when your lack of self-control has "broken walls down"? What happened?

_____
_____
_____
_____
_____

Can you think of a time when your self-control "restored walls"? What happened?

_____
_____
_____
_____
_____

Who are the most consistent people in your life? Can you think of 5 people you admire for their emotional consistency?

1. _____
2. _____
3. _____
4. _____
5. _____

What does their emotional consistency mean to you?

_____
_____
_____
_____
_____

To Sum It Up

✞ Kingdom values do not match the values of American culture.
✞ God honors patience and self-control.
✞ Consistency is a rare and precious gift worth striving to develop.
✞ Speed does not always win and is not always of greatest importance.

Meditation Moment

Sit comfortably and take three deep breaths.

Breathe in through your nose and breathe out through your mouth.

Allow your body to calm down.

Then, in this relaxed state, repeat:

With the Holy Spirit within me I am patient, calm, confident and in control of my feelings.

Breathe in and out.

With the Holy Spirit within me I am patient, calm, confident and in control of my feelings.

Breathe in and out.

With the Holy Spirit within me I am patient, calm, confident and in control of my feelings.

Breathe in and out.

Then thank God for developing these traits in you.

Action Items

✞ Record this week's memory verse on your phone (any voice recording app will do) in your own voice and listen to it three times throughout your day. Speak slowly as you record. As you listen to the recording, try following along with your own recorded voice.
✞ Practice the Meditation Moment exercise every day for the rest of the week. Notice how it affects you.

continued

Action Items (cont.)

✝ The next time you feel impatient, remember the person you identified today whose patience you admire. Ask God to help you be more like them in the area of patience..

✝ Look for people in your life who are practicing self-control. You know this isn't easy. Tell them what you see in them and complement them on having such an excellent handle on their emotions when the time is right.

EIC = ENCOUNTER + IDENTIFIED BEHAVIOR + COURSE CORRECT

Daily EIC Reflection

ENCOUNTER (E)

Describe one Christ Encounter you had today on the lines below. What happened? Where were you? Whom did you encounter? If you're not sure which one to choose, ask the Holy Spirit to highlight one God-ordained Encounter for you.

IDENTIFIED BEHAVIOR (I)

Which behaviors can you identify? Drawing on your newfound understanding in today's lesson, which of your own personality traits and motivations were at play? What were the other person's personality traits and motivations that influenced the encounter? Describe them here:

My unique personality traits and motivations:

The other person's unique personality traits and motivations:

How did these distinct traits and motivations interact with each other? Was there a clash? Did they complement each other? Reflect on this below:

Day 3 Emotional Intelligence + Self-Control = Consistency

COURSE CORRECT (C)

How did you respond? On a Spirit scale from 1–10, how did you do? Were you able to thoughtfully respond rather than react? Did you successfully surrender to God's will and course correct before you took action? Is there anything you wish you had done differently? Remember that we are going for *progress over perfection*. We are all here to learn and grow. Which lessons would you like to take with you going forward? What did you learn? Reflect on your answers to these questions below:

FLESH 1   2   3   4   5   6   7   8   9   10 SPIRIT

....

....

....

....

....

QUOTE FOR THE DAY

"Jesus always has the right to ask the question, 'Do you love me?' He did not ask Peter if he feared him, respected him, or admired him but he asked, 'Do you love me?' Jesus wants to see evidence that you love him. Jesus says, 'Inasmuch as you have done it unto one of the least of these you have done it unto me' (Matthew 25:40). Jesus says that how you treat other people is how you treat Him." (EIC, p. 115)

"Like Peter, all of us have given Jesus good reason to doubt our sincerity. We all fall short—sometimes in soul-shaming ways that we can hardly admit to ourselves—let alone to the one we have failed." (EIC, p. 114)

DAY 4
"DO YOU LOVE ME?"

What God's Word Says

"If you love me, keep my commandments." **(John 14:15)**

"When they had finished eating, Jesus said to Simon Peter, "Simon son of John, do you love me more than these?"

"Yes, Lord," he said, "you know that I love you."

Jesus said, "Feed my lambs." **(John 21:15).**

Pause & Reflect

Has anyone ever asked you to your face if you loved them? What was your response?

....

....

....

....

....

....

....

A PRAYER FOR TODAY

Jesus, thank you for your love for me.

I love you back.

In your holy name,

Amen

Today's Topic
DOES S/HE LOVE ME? DOES S/HE NOT?

How many movies and songs have you heard, seen, or seen advertised where this is the main premise? We are obsessed with love, infatuation, romance, attraction, and all the anxiety and excitement that go along with them. We want to love, we want to experience love, we want to fall in love, we don't want to be deprived of love, we want to be desired and loved. Desperately.

But when Jesus asks Peter, "Do you love me?" he isn't asking this from a place of insecurity, self-doubt, or neediness. Instead, he is giving Peter an opportunity to be restored. He is offering him an opportunity to rebuild the trust he broke. He is extending a hand of reconciliation paired with a commission and a lifelong calling.

When he asks Peter this question three times, he is also giving Peter the opportunity to declare who he is, who he wants to be, who he wishes he had been but wasn't able to be at the time of his betrayal. He is giving Peter another chance. Peter's emotion of fear overrode his ability to practice self-control to speak truth in the face of rejection. Jesus was after his restoration and He is after ours.

Although Peter doesn't seem to recognize the incredible generosity of this interaction in the moment, he does engage. He may be perplexed and even slightly irritated by the repeat question, but he does lean in. Only with time did he likely understand that Jesus had just publicly enacted his reinstatement into the fold.

Similarly, when Jesus asks us, "Do you love me?" we don't quite know what he is asking of us. We do not yet know what he is inviting us into, commissioning us to, or restoring us from. Still He asks. We are asked to commit before we know the cost, the itinerary, or the final destination of the trip; sign the dotted line before we get to see the ticket. But that's surrender and trust. And our lives will never be the same.

Look Inside

How easy is it for you to relinquish control and surrender to God?
- ✞ Oh, I've had a lot of practice.
- ✞ It's a challenge.
- ✞ Yikes, it terrifies me!

Day 4 "Do You Love Me?"

Have you ever surrendered a decision to God? What was the experience like? What was the outcome?

If Jesus were standing in front of you right now, asking you if you loved him, what would you say? How would you respond?

Can you think of anyone (personally or through books/stories/movies/etc.) who was excellent at surrendering to God? How can you tell?

Reflect on this word: surrender. What does it mean to you? Does it scare you? How would you define it?

To Sum It Up

- ✞ Jesus asked Peter, "Do you love me?" And Jesus asks this of you too.
- ✞ When Peter answered in the affirmative, he did not yet know what kind of life (and even death) he was committing.
- ✞ Surrender means placing our trust in God before we know the exact outcome of that decision.
- ✞ Because Christ reigns victorious, we DO know that the final outcome will be good.

Meditation Moment

Prayerfully imagine Jesus asking you three times if you love him. Picture the scene: Where is He asking you this? How is He saying it? What does it mean to you?

Then consider your response: How will you reply? Which words will you choose? What's your tone of voice? What is your body language saying? How do you feel?

> ### Action Items
>
> - ✞ Listen to your recording of this week's Bible verse again. Now try reciting it from memory (without the recording). Can you do it? Don't forget to quote the reference. Keep practicing it until you feel confident.
> - ✞ Take whatever God revealed to you during the Meditation Moment and commit it to memory.
> - ✞ The next time you're afraid or feel out of control, commit your request to God in prayer. Be real with Him. Then surrender your will to His.
> - ✞ Commit to loving the Lord your God with all your heart, soul, mind, and strength.

EIC = ENCOUNTER + IDENTIFIED BEHAVIOR + COURSE CORRECT

Daily EIC Reflection

ENCOUNTER (E)

Describe one Christ Encounter you had today on the lines below. What happened? Where were you? Whom did you encounter? If you're not sure which one to choose, ask the Holy Spirit to highlight one God-ordained Encounter for you.

IDENTIFIED BEHAVIOR (I)

Which behaviors can you identify? Drawing on your newfound understanding in today's lesson, which of your own personality traits and motivations were at play? What were the other person's personality traits and motivations that influenced the encounter? Describe them here:

My unique personality traits and motivations:

The other person's unique personality traits and motivations:

How did these distinct traits and motivations interact with each other? Was there a clash? Did they complement each other? Reflect on this below:

COURSE CORRECT (C)

How did you respond? On a Spirit scale from 1–10, how did you do? Were you able to thoughtfully respond rather than react? Did you successfully surrender to God's will and course correct before you took action? Is there anything you wish you had done differently? Remember that we are going for *progress over perfection*. We are all here to learn and grow. Which lessons would you like to take with you going forward? What did you learn? Reflect on your answers to these questions below:

| 1 | 2 | 3 | 4 | 5 | 6 | 7 | 8 | 9 | 10 |

_____
_____
_____
_____
_____
_____
_____
_____
_____

QUOTE FOR THE DAY

"When we 'abide' in Jesus, according to John 15:5, we will bear much fruit. Great results personally and with others will flow out of our relationship with Jesus. Further, when we fail to 'abide' or remain in Jesus, our source, Scripture says that we 'can do nothing.'" (EIC, p. 86–87)

"We are guaranteed that by being close to Jesus, we will experience hardship. However, He promises to provide comfort and peace through His Spirit and the ability to overcome temptation with self-control." (EIC, p. 87)

"Your great challenge in developing self-control and leading like Jesus is that your human ego causes you to try and attain the worthiness of the unconditional love that is already yours. It hurts your pride to accept that you cannot increase God's love for you by anything you do. He loves you totally and unconditionally as much today as he ever has or ever will. He cannot love you more; his love for you is perfect. It is breathtaking to even get a glimpse of how much he loves you and what it cost him." (EIC, p. 112)

Day 5

ABIDING IN GOD'S UNCONDITIONAL LOVE

What God's Word Says

"Remain in me, as I also remain in you. No branch can bear fruit by itself; it must remain in the vine. Neither can you bear fruit unless you remain in me. I am the vine; you are the branches. If you remain in me and I in you, you will bear much fruit; apart from me you can do nothing." **(John 15:4–5)**

> Surely your goodness and love will follow me
> > all the days of my life,
> > and I will dwell in the house of the Lord
> > forever. **(Psalm 23:6)**

Pause & Reflect

What do you associate with the word, "abide"? How does it make you feel?

A Prayer for Today

God, it really is breathtaking to get a glimpse of how much you love me. Thank you for your profound, faithful, overwhelming love for me. Please help me to not just accept and receive it but to actually abide in it, inhabit it, and rest in it. Help me to remain in you so that I have victory in the area of self-controlling my emotions and behavior.

I love you too.

In Jesus's name,

Amen

Today's Topic
CAN I HANG OUT JUST A LITTLE WHILE LONGER?

What are some of your favorite places to hang out? And what is it about them that makes you so comfortable? Is it the people? The atmosphere? The music? The memories? The sounds and smells? The vibe?

Some of us have certain places we like to return to over and over. Places we never want to leave. They give us a sense of familiarity and comfort; there is a warm glow around them; they revive something in us; they nourish our soul.

God wants to be such a place for us. His love is the ultimate restoration of our souls. When we are nurtured and sustained on a level no one and nothing else can offer us, why would we ever want to leave?

Can you picture a child pulling on their dad's pant leg and whining, "But do we *have to*? Do we really have to go?" When we make our home in God, He can become our comforting, safe, reassuring place. A place we can return to over and over.

In fact, we're always invited and we never have to leave.

Look Inside

Where are some places you love to hang out?

....
....
....
....
....

Have you ever considered "abiding" in God as hanging out with Him? Does this resonate with you or not? Why (not)?

....
....
....
....
....

Day 5 Abiding in God's Unconditional Love

Do you like hanging out with/abiding in God?
- ✝ Oh yes, it's the best!
- ✝ Yeah, sometimes.
- ✝ Uh, he's kind of a bore.
- ✝ I'm not sure what you mean.

When have you experienced a strong sense of God's presence in your life? When that happened, did you want to hurry up and leave? What was it like? Describe it in as much detail as you like.

Are there any practices you can think of that help you "abide"? What are they? List them here:

What have you noticed to be different when it comes to your ability to practice self-control over your emotions and behaviors after you spend time with God? List them here:

_____
_____
_____
_____
_____
_____
_____
_____
_____
_____

To Sum It Up

- ✞ Abiding in God can be the most restful, reassuring thing.
- ✞ Although abiding in God may not look like "work," it is necessary for a fruitful life.
- ✞ God's love for you is perfect.
- ✞ King David didn't want to leave God's presence (Psalm 23); because of Jesus's work on the cross, we don't have to.

Meditation Moment

Please pray this adaptation of John 15:4–5:

Lord, I desire to remain in you, as you ask me to. I know I cannot bear the fruit of self-control on my own but must remain in you if I want to discern and manage my emotions and behavior in a way that honors you by loving others well. You, Lord, are the vine, and I am a branch. I believe you when you say that if I remain in you, I will bear much fruit and if I do not, I can do nothing. Please sustain me—help me to remain in you faithfully so that I will bear abundant fruit.

In Jesus's name,

Amen

Action Items

✟ Write this week's Bible verse out from memory on the lines below. Don't cheat! Once you have written it out and reviewed it, go back and check it with your handwritten original. How did you do?

_____
_____
_____
_____

✟ The next time you're in prayer, try stretching it just a little bit longer. Is there something more God may want to tell you?
✟ Play some worship music and practice simply *being* in God's presence without *doing* anything for Him.
✟ Do less, rest more.

EIC = ENCOUNTER + IDENTIFIED BEHAVIOR + COURSE CORRECT

Daily EIC Reflection

ENCOUNTER (E)

Describe one Christ Encounter you had today on the lines below. What happened? Where were you? Whom did you encounter? If you're not sure which one to choose, ask the Holy Spirit to highlight one God-ordained Encounter for you.

_____
_____
_____
_____
_____
_____
_____

IDENTIFIED BEHAVIOR (I)

Which behaviors can you identify? Drawing on your newfound understanding in today's lesson, which of your own personality traits and motivations were at play? What were the other person's personality traits and motivations that influenced the encounter? Describe them here:

My unique personality traits and motivations:

The other person's unique personality traits and motivations:

How did these distinct traits and motivations interact with each other? Was there a clash? Did they complement each other? Reflect on this below:

COURSE CORRECT (C)

How did you respond? On a Spirit scale from 1–10, how did you do? Were you able to thoughtfully respond rather than react? Did you successfully surrender to God's will and course correct before you took action? Is there anything you wish you had done differently?

Remember that we are going for *progress over perfection*. We are all here to learn and grow. Which lessons would you like to take with you going forward? What did you learn? Reflect on your answers to these questions below:

1   2   3   4   5   6   7   8   9   10

_____
_____
_____
_____
_____
_____
_____
_____
_____

Intro to Week 4
Altruistic Attitude
(Social Awareness)

MEMORY VERSE FOR THE WEEK

"You call me 'Teacher' and 'Lord,' and rightly so, for that is what I am. Now that I, your Lord and Teacher, have washed your feet, you also should wash one another's feet. I have set you an example that you should do as I have done for you" (John 13:13–15).

A SUPPORT RESOURCE FOR THE WEEK TO EXPLORE

Edge God In Podcast: Exploring Altruism Part 1
https://edgegodin.com/exploring-altruism-part-1-gods-altruistic-intention-for-humanity/

Welcome Message

Welcome to Week 4, where we will focus on loving your neighbor as yourself.

There is no way around the fact that our relationship with God has immediate ramifications for our relationships with our (physical and metaphorical) neighbors. Drawing close to God will invariably transform us and therefore change our relationships with others. This week we will investigate what it means to love your neighbor as yourself, focus on drawing near to God, and explore our relationship with self, others, and Christ. We will then zoom out and look at how these relate to one another in the wider Christian ecosystem of relationships—the body of Christ. Finally, we will investigate the meaning of appropriate altruism.

As we've said before, please engage this process as deeply as possible. Just like any program or tool, you get out of it what you put into it. Allow yourself to be challenged by the questions and reflection opportunities contained here. Allow yourself to be stretched and grow. Enjoy this opportunity to intentionally set aside time for spiritual renewal.

We hope this week's study will encourage you to love your neighbor well, draw closer to God, and actively contribute to a healthy Christian community.

Connecting Hearts in Him,

Estella, Lauren, and Rich

ALTRUISTIC ATTITUDE/SOCIAL AWARENESS WEEK 4

QUOTE FOR THE DAY

"Have you ever noticed the joy, purpose, and peace you experience when you do a random act of kindness for another person? That is God's love in action, the simple definition of altruism and your greatest place of purpose." (EIC, p. 132)

"Don't let the troubles of this world affect the sharing of God's love." (EIC, p. 132)

DAY 1
LOVING YOUR NEIGHBOR AS YOURSELF

What God's Word Says

"Do nothing out of selfish ambition or vain conceit. Rather, in humility value others above yourselves, not looking to your own interests but each of you to the interests of the others. You must have the same attitude as Christ" **(Philippians 2:3–5).**

On one occasion an expert in the law stood up to test Jesus. "Teacher," he asked, "what must I do to inherit eternal life?"

"What is written in the Law?" he replied. "How do you read it?"

He answered, "'Love the Lord your God with all your heart and with all your soul and with all your strength and with all your mind'; and, 'Love your neighbor as yourself.'"

"You have answered correctly," Jesus replied. "Do this and you will live."

But he wanted to justify himself, so he asked Jesus, "And who is my neighbor?"

In reply Jesus said: "A man was going down from Jerusalem to Jericho, when he was attacked by robbers. They stripped him of his clothes, beat him and went away, leaving him half dead. A priest happened to be going down the same road, and when he saw the man, he passed by on the other side. So too, a Levite, when he came to the place and saw him, passed by on the other side. But a Samaritan, as he traveled, came where the man was; and when he saw him, he took pity on him. He went to him and bandaged his wounds, pouring on oil and wine. Then he put the man on his own donkey, brought him to an inn and took care of him. The next day he took out two denarii and gave them to the innkeeper. 'Look after him,' he said, 'and when I return, I will reimburse you for any extra expense you may have.'

"Which of these three do you think was a neighbor to the man who fell into the hands of robbers?"

The expert in the law replied, "The one who had mercy on him."

Jesus told him, "Go and do likewise" (Luke 10:25-37).

Pause & Reflect

Having read Jesus's response to the question, how would you answer the question, "And who is my neighbor?"

....
....
....
....
....
....
....
....
....
....

A PRAYER FOR TODAY

Lord, you created each one of us. Thank you. And we all bear your image. Thank you for making this planet so diverse. Thank you for making us so different. Thank you that your love and your heart are big enough to embrace every culture, every tribe, and every tongue on earth. You are truly amazing.

Please forgive us for drawing artificial lines in the sand and deciding who is "in" and who is "out." Teach us, please, how to see and love our neighbors, whether they look, act, and speak like us or not. Give us creativity, Holy Spirit, and teach us how to love as you love.

In Jesus's name,

Amen

Today's Topic
LOVING YOUR NEIGHBOR, JESUS-STYLE

Control. We like it. *Who's in? Who's out? Who's on my team? Who's for me? Who likes me? Who's against me? Do I have any competition in the room? How many followers do I have? How do I look? How do I sound? Am I winning?*

We like to know how we stack up against others, how we rank, how we are perceived, and whether we are good enough. In the eyes of others, in our own eyes, and even in the eyes of God. When the expert in the law approached Jesus, he "wanted to justify himself." He wanted to know the outer limits of how far his love had to reach to please God. But Jesus flips the question on him. Rather than answer the question, "Who is my neighbor?" Jesus tells a parable, then concludes it with a very different question: "Which of these three do you think was a neighbor to the man who fell into the hands of robbers?"

By telling the parable, Jesus redirects the listeners' attention and lets us know the expert was asking the wrong question altogether! Rather than use the "neighbor" label on a limited and specified number of people, Jesus shifts the conversation toward the Samaritan's behavior. Who's *acting* like a neighbor in this story? As Mr. Rogers might say, "Where are the helpers?"[1] He doesn't focus on whether the injured and violated man was worthy, ceremonially clean, popular, wealthy, holy, or in any other way deserving. Instead, he focuses on who shows up for him in his time of need. And oh, right, in this case it's someone the expert would not have considered his neighbor at all!

With this story Jesus is blowing the limits way off our conventional understandings of who we consider one of our own. This pairs well with the Genesis account of our creation, one takeaway of which is: *We're all related!*[2] Rather than focus on who is in and who is out, Jesus leaves us with a challenge to "go and do likewise." To lavish generosity on others, whether they are in the "in" crowd or not. To see people, recognize their need, love them, and act. Even if it costs us. Emotional Intelligence in Christ speaks to a love that steps away from our own personal needs to own, control and possess the behavior of people around us and calls us to love as Jesus loves even when we don't feel like it. This is a job for Jesus.

Look Inside

What are some of the obstacles that keep you from going and doing likewise? Have you ever overcome them? Write the story down. What went well? What didn't?

Day 1 Loving Your Neighbor as Yourself

Generally speaking, would you say it's easy for you to love your neighbor as yourself?
- ♰ Oh yes, it's natural!
- ♰ Depends on the day.
- ♰ To be honest, it's tough.
- ♰ Impossible!

Is there anyone God might want you to consider your neighbor that you would rather not love? Talk to God about this person. What does God have to say about them? Is there anything He'd like you to know about them?

Pick at least three people God highlights for you. What are their names? Commit to praying for them this week.

How can you practically go about loving your neighbor as yourself? List five ways you can think of:

1.
2.
3.
4.
5.

Take some time to ask God who he wants you to love today. As you listen, who comes up? Are there any surprises?

To Sum It Up

- ✞ If we want to worship God, loving our neighbor is not optional.
- ✞ "Whatever you did for one of the least of these brothers and sisters of mine, you did for me."
- ✞ Focus on *being* a neighbor (to all) rather than figuring out who to include in your in-group of neighbors.
- ✞ Sometimes "the helpers" are not who you may have expected. Be open to being surprised and seeing people in a new light.

Meditation Moment

Imagine a world in which everyone realized they were everybody else's small-town neighbor. A world in which everyone knew they'd have to see each other again the next day. And how they treated you would get out in the gossip around town. And how you treated them mattered and would be remembered for generations. What would that world be like?

Action Items

- ✞ Read this week's memory verse (along with the reference where it can be found) three times and manually write it out here:

  _____
  _____
  _____

- ✞ Do you know your physical neighbors? If not, pray for a (natural, safe) opportunity to meet them and introduce yourself. Listen for ways you can be a blessing to them.
- ✞ As you listen to your friends and relatives talk, pay special attention to hints they might drop: What is causing them anxiety? What worries them? What brings them joy? Just start by noticing these things and making mental notes.
- ✞ Ask God if there is anything He would like you to do in response to things you noticed about the people around you. Ask the Holy Spirit for love, creativity, and guidance. Then joyfully obey.

Day 1 Loving Your Neighbor as Yourself

EIC = ENCOUNTER + IDENTIFIED BEHAVIOR + COURSE CORRECT

Daily EIC Reflection

ENCOUNTER (E)

Describe one Christ Encounter you had today on the lines below. What happened? Where were you? Whom did you encounter? If you're not sure which one to choose, ask the Holy Spirit to highlight one God-ordained Encounter for you.

_____
_____
_____
_____
_____
_____
_____
_____
_____

IDENTIFIED BEHAVIOR (I)

What behaviors did you act out? Drawing on your newfound understanding in today's lesson, which of your own personality traits and motivations were at play? What were the other person's personality traits and motivations that influenced the encounter? Describe them here:

My unique personality traits and motivations:

_____
_____
_____

The other person's unique personality traits and motivations:

_____
_____
_____

How did these distinct traits and motivations interact with each other? Was there a clash? Did they complement each other? Reflect on this below:

COURSE CORRECT (C)

How did you respond? On a Spirit scale from 1–10, how did you do? Were you able to thoughtfully respond rather than react? Did you successfully surrender to God's will and course correct before you took action? Is there anything you wish you had done differently? Remember that we are going for *progress over perfection*. We are all here to learn and grow. Which lessons would you like to take with you going forward? What did you learn? Reflect on your answers to these questions below:

QUOTE FOR THE DAY

"God went further to create human beings with the deliberate intention of having us experience and express the love that exists between the Father, Son, and Holy Spirit." (EIC, p. 126)

"An essential reflection here is to fill up with the intimacy of God first. Then from that overflow of encountering God's love, you are in a position to love your neighbor in a healthy portion, without depleting yourself." (EIC, p. 128)

"As you sift out the motives fueled by self-interest, you set yourself free to offer a pure gift of selfless concern for another person, which in turn allows you to see God." (EIC, p. 138)

DAY 2
INTIMACY WITH GOD

What God's Word Says

"Search me, God, and know my heart; test me and know my anxious thoughts. See if there is any offensive way in me and lead me in the way everlasting" (**Psalm 139:23–24**).

"Blessed are the pure in heart, for they shall see God" (**Matthew 5:8**).

Pause & Reflect

On a scale from 1 to 10, how close would you say you are to God? How open are you with Him? Is it easy for you to open up to Him or is that a challenge?

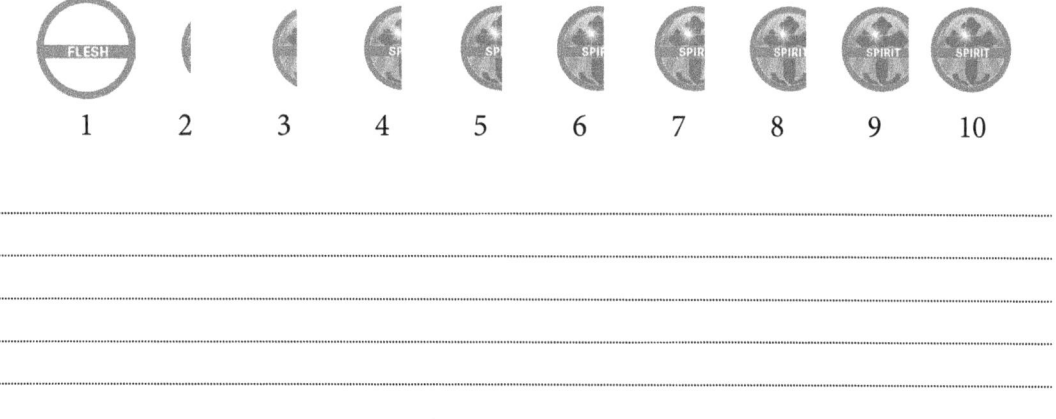

....
....
....
....

Altruistic Attitude/Social Awareness Week 4

A PRAYER FOR TODAY

Lord, I love you. Thank you so much for loving me first. Please draw me close to you. I want to remain in communion with you as Jesus did. I want to be so connected with you that I am aware of your every move and only do as you say. I want to know your heart so well that my actions reflect it. Thank you for revealing yourself to me, God, and thank you for drawing me close.

In Jesus's name,

Amen

Today's Topic
INTIMACY IS WHAT IT'S ALL ABOUT

You may have heard the saying that the longest journey we take is the one from our head to our heart.³ When the psalmist prays, "Search me, God, and know my heart," he is inviting God into the deepest, most personal parts of his being. He's saying, "Don't stay out there, come on in. Look around. Let me show you everything." Although we sometimes dismiss it, devalue it, or relegate it to the sidelines of our lives, intimacy is the very core of our spiritual life. It is also of great value to God.

We see this in the way Jesus interacted with people, recorded throughout the gospels. Whether it was seeing Philip under the fig tree, addressing the woman at the well, calling out to Zacchaeus, or asking Mary why she was weeping in the garden of Gethsemane, Jesus expressed a tender care that made them and makes us feel deeply seen and known.

But intimacy with God is not only reserved for the New Testament. In Genesis 16:13 Hagar declares, "You are the God who sees me," after seeing and hearing from the angel of the Lord. He saw her in her distress and revealed her future to her, clearly having an intimate knowledge of her life. When Abraham was about to sacrifice his son Isaac in obedience to God (Genesis 22), the angel of the Lord did not only stop him from doing so but also provided an animal to be sacrificed in his stead. When God called Abram and told him to "Go from your country, your people and your father's household to the land I will show you," (Genesis 12:1) God was not just asking Abram to step out in faith and trust (though He certainly was), he was also saying: "I know you. I hold your future. I know what is best for you. Therefore: Trust me."

Trust without intimacy is just blind trust. It's naïve and often very unwise. But God invites us into an intimate relationship with him that allows us to truly get to know him. And once we do, we realize that trusting Him is the most logical, safest, and most predictable choice. Not because the journeys He invites us on are predictable (they are *not*!) but because God remains the same yesterday, today, and forever (Hebrews 13:8) and staying close to Him and remaining in His will is the very best place to be. He knows that we cannot give out to the people around us what we have not experienced within.

Look Inside

When have you felt particularly close to God? What do you remember about that time? Try to remember as many details as possible:

When have you felt particularly far from God? What was going on during that time? What do you remember? (Again, be as detailed as possible.)

What are the top 5 things that help you connect to God and then the people around you in a way that honors God? (You could list people, places, practices . . . anything you like.)

1.
2.
3.
4.
5.

Can you describe what it feels like to you to be close to God? What's it like? Try putting into words.

Read Psalm 139 through the lens of intimacy. What do you notice?

To Sum It Up

- ✞ If we focus on intimacy with God first, we can give to our neighbor without burning out.
- ✞ Intimacy with God is the very core of our spiritual life.
- ✞ Jesus deeply knows and sees you.
- ✞ Abraham and Hagar knew God intimately.

Meditation Moment

Think about how a head of lettuce grows. It grows from its "heart"—from the inside out. The leaves grow and mature and gradually become the outer layers while inner layers keep on reproducing, protected by the older, more weathered leaves on the outside.

Deer love to come along and pluck these "hearts" right out of the lettuce plant because they are the sweetest, freshest leaves. But once they are gone, the lettuce plant can no longer grow; it's lost its core—it's hollow on the inside. Although the more mature leaves may still be on the plant, and it may look alive on the outside, the plant is no longer growing; it is virtually dead.

Your spiritual life is no different.

Action Items

✝ Read this week's memory verse out loud three times, each time trying to commit more of it to memory. Think about what it means and why each of the words were chosen when it was originally written. Create any memory aids you can think of. Rather than read it in print, read your own handwritten version (from yesterday) to help you memorize it.

✝ As you pray, make an extra effort to keep it real. Where you might usually hold back an emotion or a word, try not doing so. See how God responds.

✝ Make a point of intentionally doing one of the things you listed that help you connect with God this week.

✝ Intimacy is about listening too. Keep a journal and listen to what God is saying to you today. Write it down so you won't forget. Look for opportunities to make a conscious effort to hear what people are saying to you. Listen to understand rather than to be understood.

EIC = ENCOUNTER + IDENTIFIED BEHAVIOR + COURSE CORRECT

Daily EIC Reflection

ENCOUNTER (E)

Describe one Christ Encounter you had today on the lines below. What happened? Where were you? Whom did you encounter? If you're not sure which one to choose, ask the Holy Spirit to highlight one God-ordained Encounter for you.

_____
_____
_____
_____
_____
_____
_____
_____
_____
_____

IDENTIFIED BEHAVIOR (I)

What behaviors did you act out? Drawing on your newfound understanding in today's lesson, which of your own personality traits and motivations were at play? What were the other person's personality traits and motivations that influenced the encounter? Describe them here:

My unique personality traits and motivations:

....
....
....
....
....

The other person's unique personality traits and motivations:

....
....
....
....
....

How did these distinct traits and motivations interact with each other? Was there a clash? Did they complement each other? Reflect on this below:

....
....
....
....
....

COURSE CORRECT (C)

How did you respond? On a Spirit scale from 1–10, how did you do? Were you able to thoughtfully respond rather than react? Did you successfully surrender to God's will and course correct before you took action? Is there anything you wish you had done differently? Remember that we are going for *progress over perfection*. We are all here to learn and grow. Which lessons would you like to take with you going forward? What did you learn? Reflect on your answers to these questions below:

1 2 3 4 5 6 7 8 9 10

_____
_____
_____
_____
_____
_____
_____
_____

QUOTE FOR THE DAY

"As immortal spirits, we are made in God's image, housed in the flesh, with his characteristics. This sets us apart from other animals because we have the remarkable ability to relate to God." (EIC, p. 127)

"Mark 12:31 says: 'Love your neighbor as yourself.' This also means you will never love another any more than you love yourself. And you will only love yourself when you know you are loved by God, which leads you to care for yourself." (EIC, p. 129)

"Being altruistic can be supported by having a relationship with self, others, and first and foremost, Christ. An association of all three (God, self, others) involves developing the awareness, discernment, emotion, and renewal needed for effective Christ-filled relationships." (EIC, p. 139)

DAY 3
BEING IN RELATIONSHIP WITH SELF, OTHERS, AND CHRIST

What God's Word Says

"Love the Lord your God with all your heart and with all your soul and with all your strength and with all your mind; and, love your neighbor as yourself" **(Luke 10:27)**.

"Be devoted to one another in love. Honor one another above yourselves" **(Romans 12:10)**.

Pause & Reflect

Of these three relationships (self, others, God), which do you think is healthiest in your life? Which of them do you think is least healthy at the moment?

....

....

....

....

A PRAYER FOR TODAY

Lord, I come to you today, asking you to renew my relationship with myself, others, and you. Please put each of these relationships in the right perspective. My perspective gets so easily distorted and my priorities get jumbled. I don't want to value any of these relationships too much or too little. Please restore and heal my relationship with myself. Please restore and heal my relationships with others. And please restore and heal my relationship with you.

In Jesus's name,

Amen

Today's Topic
LOVING GOD, SELF, AND NEIGHBOR

What is it that ties our love for neighbor together with our love for God? According to the Bible, they are inextricable. Love for God is expressed, to a great extent, in our love for our neighbor. James makes it very clear that "faith by itself, if it is not accompanied by action, is dead." (James 2:17) And the actions he uses in his examples have everything to do with how we love our (more vulnerable) neighbors. Love for God—if it is sincere—and being beloved of God—if we let God's love in—automatically overflow into love for our neighbor.

Similarly, a healthy relationship with God helps us love ourselves. Although there is no verse in the Bible that expressly admonishes us to "love thyself," a healthy self-love is implied throughout. The Scriptures assume that we will care for our body, respect ourselves, and want what is best for those we love—including ourselves. The psalmist exclaims in wonder: "I praise you because I am fearfully and wonderfully made!" (Psalm 139:14) This joyful exclamation is an expression of gratitude to God as well as a healthy self-love, self-esteem, and self-appreciation. It is not selfish to love ourselves; it's healthy. Just not to the exclusion of God and neighbor. Our ability to discern and manage our emotions and behaviors in a way that honors God by loving others well as Jesus did (Emotional Intelligence in Christ) flows directly from our own personal encounter with God's immense and great love for us.

With all of our emphasis on humility, this message can sometimes get lost. But without knowing ourselves and loving ourselves, we truly have nothing to give. Jesus was able to empty himself of his divinity and die on the cross for us precisely because he knew exactly who He was and never lost touch with the Father. It is the intimacy we reflected on yesterday that allows for such a healthy and accurate view of ourselves.

In Romans 12:3 we are admonished to gain a healthy view of ourselves— not to value ourselves too highly but not to devalue ourselves either: "Do not think of yourself more highly than you ought, but rather think of yourself with sober judgment, in accordance with the faith God has distributed to each of you." Perhaps humility is, as C.S. Lewis declared in Mere Christianity, to not to think less of yourself but to think of yourself less.

And always it comes back to God. Back to how God sees us, the gifts God has given us, and the value God has placed in us by adopting us into his family. It is possible for us to be self-full without being full of ourselves. In fact, it may be necessary and important for us to have something authentic and meaningful to offer God, ourselves, and the world.

LOOK INSIDE

Would you consider yourself self-full?
- ✞ Oh yes, absolutely!
- ✞ Maybe?
- ✞ I'm not sure that's allowed.
- ✞ I'm not sure I know what you mean.

Have you ever experienced a healthy relationship with yourself bubble over into healthier relationships with others? What do you remember? How did that happen?

_____
_____
_____
_____

Have you ever experienced a healthy relationship with God bubble over into healthier relationships with others? What do you remember? How did that happen?

_____
_____
_____
_____

Have you ever experienced a healthy relationship with others bubble over into a healthier relationship with yourself? What do you remember? How did that happen?

_____
_____
_____
_____

Have you ever experienced a healthy relationship with others bubble over into a healthier relationship with God? What do you remember? How did that happen?

_____
_____

Reflecting on your answers above, what do you notice?

To Sum It Up

✝ Our relationships with self, others, and God are very much related and can mutually enrich each other.

✝ A healthy/healed relationship with ourselves is of great importance.

✝ Allowing ourselves to feel God's love for us benefits all of our relationships.

✝ It is best to view ourselves with sober (accurate) judgment—neither inflating nor deflating ourselves.

Meditation Moment

Please pray this adaptation of Luke 10:27:

Lord, today I commit to loving you with all my heart, all my soul, all my strength, and all my mind. I also commit to loving my neighbor as myself. Empower me, please, to truly and consistently love myself, others, and you.

In Jesus's name,

Amen

Action Items

✝ Record this week's memory verse on your phone (any voice recording app will do) in your own voice and listen to it three times throughout your day. Speak slowly as you record. As you listen to the recording, try following along with your own recorded voice.

continued

Action Items (cont.)

✝ Write down five things you love about yourself.

_____

_____

_____

_____

✝ Call some of your closest friends and ask them what they love about you. Add their words to your list.

✝ Thank God for making you as He did. Show up to your relationships with God and others self-full: as your true self remembering you can't give out what you have not experienced within.

EIC = ENCOUNTER + IDENTIFIED BEHAVIOR + COURSE CORRECT

DAILY EIC REFLECTION

ENCOUNTER (E)

Describe one Christ Encounter you had today on the lines below. What happened? Where were you? Whom did you encounter? If you're not sure which one to choose, ask the Holy Spirit to highlight one God-ordained Encounter for you.

_____

_____

_____

_____

_____

_____

_____

_____

IDENTIFIED BEHAVIOR (I)

What behaviors did you act out? Drawing on your newfound understanding in today's lesson, which of your own personality traits and motivations were at play? What were the other person's personality traits and motivations that influenced the encounter? Describe them here:

My unique personality traits and motivations:

The other person's unique personality traits and motivations:

How did these distinct traits and motivations interact with each other? Was there a clash? Did they complement each other? Reflect on this below:

COURSE CORRECT (C)

How did you respond? On a Spirit scale from 1–10, how did you do? Were you able to thoughtfully respond rather than react? Did you successfully surrender to God's will and course correct before you took action? Is there anything you wish you had done differently? Remember that we are going for *progress over perfection*. We are all here to learn and grow. Which lessons would you like to take with you going forward? What did you learn? Reflect on your answers to these questions below:

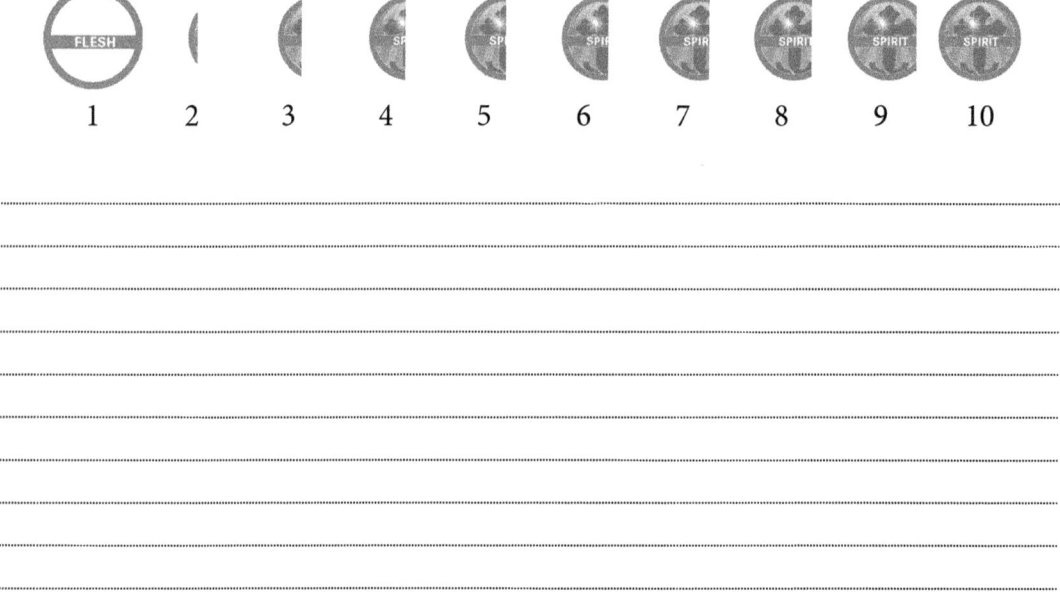

QUOTE FOR THE DAY

"Remember that we are an important element of Christ's ecosystem, His community. The body of Christ ecosystem is made up of several different kinds of communities sharing resources that help each survive in a more cooperative environment. Ecosystems shouldn't work in silos but rather in unity toward God's strategy [. . .] for now, concentrate your thoughts on the role you play individually to support the growth and strength of God's ecosystem as a whole. Remember that the whole is greater than the sum of its parts, and that each part must continually work toward the altruistic nature He desires for us." (EIC, p. 129–130)

Day 4
THE CHRISTIAN ECOSYSTEM

What God's Word Says

"For just as each of us has one body with many members, and these members do not all have the same function, so in Christ we, though many, form one body, and each member belongs to all the others. We have different gifts, according to the grace given to each of us. If your gift is prophesying, then prophesy in accordance with your faith; if it is serving, then serve; if it is teaching, then teach; if it is to encourage, then give encouragement; if it is giving, then give generously; if it is to lead, do it diligently; if it is to show mercy, do it cheerfully" **(Romans 12:4–8)**.

Pause & Reflect

Are you currently plugged in to a Christian community? What do you think makes for a healthy Christian ecosystem?

....
....
....
....
....
....
....
....

A PRAYER FOR TODAY

Lord, I confess that I try to be self-sufficient a lot. I don't like to rely on others for anything. I like to think of my relationship with you as being personal, private, just between you and me. But I know that is not healthy and I would like to grow into Christian community the way you envision it. What does a healthy Christian ecosystem look like, God? If I'm not in one yet, please help me either find, actively contribute to, or start one.

In Jesus's name,

Amen

Today's Topic
HEALTHY INTERDEPENDENCE IN THE KINGDOM OF GOD

1 Corinthians 12 presents us with a beautiful image of the Christian ecosystem:

> The eye cannot say to the hand, "I don't need you!" And the head cannot say to the feet, "I don't need you!" On the contrary, those parts of the body that seem to be weaker are indispensable, and the parts that we think are less honorable we treat with special honor. And the parts that are unpresentable are treated with special modesty, while our presentable parts need no special treatment. But God has put the body together, giving greater honor to the parts that lacked it, so that there should be no division in the body, but that its parts should have equal concern for each other. If one part suffers, every part suffers with it; if one part is honored, every part rejoices with it.

This is the example by which we are to live. Although we live in a time in which the illusion of self-sufficiency is popular and we may even be able to fool ourselves into thinking that "God and I" is enough, this is not the biblical picture of a fulfilled Christian life. No matter how highly esteemed any of our individual gifts may be (or not), we are still in need of others to complete and complement us in the body of Christ. The life of faith is best lived in community. We wouldn't want to go without one another's gifts—we would be depriving ourselves! We are at our healthiest when we are an interdependent ecosystem.

Imagine a worship service that was made up of only a sermon. Or only a Scripture reading. Or only worship music. Holy Communion without any preparation or reconciliation. Or only the passing of the peace. Or only the benediction. Would the service be complete? And these are all visible parts of the service! What about a worship service without anyone having cleaned the bathrooms? Without anyone running the sound booth? Without anyone to greet you at the door? How would that affect your experience? Each one of these elements is important and contributes something significant to the worship service. Without them, it's just not the same.

Likewise, imagine if one person tried to do them all. Imagine the pastor trying to greet you at the door, then lead the music, jump up to give the sermon, administer Holy Communion, clean up the church, intersperse sound checks, and then send you on your way with the benediction.

No doubt there are some churches who rely on a very small number of people to lead the church. But there is no reason to sit on the sidelines and let others do it all. Your gifts are needed. Just as every part of the service is important and every part of the body needs to work together with the other parts to keep a body healthy, your contribution matters. Whether you are preaching from the pulpit or cleaning the bathrooms, we need you. Your contribution is valuable and keeps the whole church running.

Experiencing for ourselves that our contribution matters and helps the church thrive can add great joy to our lives.

Look Inside

Have you ever been part of a thriving Christian ecosystem? How did you know?

....
....
....
....

Have you ever been part of a Christian ecosystem that was struggling to stay alive? Or just barely getting by? What were the tell-tale signs? How did you know?

....
....
....
....

On a scale from 1 to 10, how connected to Christian community are you right now?

| 1 | 2 | 3 | 4 | 5 | 6 | 7 | 8 | 9 | 10 |

If you're not in one now, what do you think it would feel like to be part of a thriving Christian ecosystem? How would that affect your faith?

....
....
....
....

Day 4 The Christian Ecosystem

Can you think of a Christian community you're familiar with that's exemplary in this department? If so, what is their name? If not, where might you find one?

....
....
....
....
....

To Sum It Up

- ✞ The body of Christ is like an ecosystem; each part is dependent on one another and the whole is greater than its parts.
- ✞ All of our gifts, no matter how flashy or humble, are valuable and needed.
- ✞ Self-sufficiency is not the answer. "God and I" is not enough.

Meditation Moment

Consider this:

I am one member on a fantastic team—the body of Christ. Together, we have a very lofty goal. I am important but not *that* important. I make my contribution; I matter, as do others. I couldn't do my job without all of my other team members and they rely on me to do my job too. In fact, we all rely on each other. There's no other way we could ever reach our goal!

Action Items

- ✞ Listen to your recording of this week's Bible verse again. Now try reciting it from memory (without the recording). Can you do it? Don't forget to quote the reference. Keep practicing it until you feel confident.
- ✞ Be on the lookout for an opportunity to express a need to someone in a safe way. It may be in a group setting or a 1:1 conversation. Sharing a need is vulnerable and can open the door to mutual interdependence. It takes courage too!
- ✞ Practice graciously accepting help. Practice generously offering help.
- ✞ Be mindful of spending at least as much time in intercession for others as you do for yourself and your own needs.

EIC = ENCOUNTER + IDENTIFIED BEHAVIOR + COURSE CORRECT

Daily EIC Reflection

ENCOUNTER (E)

Describe one Christ Encounter you had today on the lines below. What happened? Where were you? Whom did you encounter? If you're not sure which one to choose, ask the Holy Spirit to highlight one God-ordained Encounter for you.

_____
_____
_____
_____
_____
_____
_____
_____
_____

IDENTIFIED BEHAVIOR (I)

What behaviors did you act out? Drawing on your newfound understanding in today's lesson, which of your own personality traits and motivations were at play? What were the other person's personality traits and motivations that influenced the encounter? Describe them here:

My unique personality traits and motivations:

_____
_____
_____
_____

The other person's unique personality traits and motivations:

_____
_____

How did these distinct traits and motivations interact with each other? Was there a clash? Did they complement each other? Reflect on this below:

COURSE CORRECT (C)

How did you respond? On a Spirit scale from 1–10, how did you do? Were you able to thoughtfully respond rather than react? Did you successfully surrender to God's will and course correct before you took action? Is there anything you wish you had done differently? Remember that we are going for *progress over perfection*. We are all here to learn and grow. Which lessons would you like to take with you going forward? What did you learn? Reflect on your answers to these questions below:

QUOTE FOR THE DAY

"It is love that moves us into the realm of emotional intelligence in Christ, and altruism is love in action." (EIC, p. 128)

"When the ego takes over, altruistic behavior is lost, and we lose sight of the teaching and love of Christ." (EIC, p. 129)

"Selfless concern for other people is made possible through our personal experience with the love of God. God's way of giving is our only example of genuine altruism." (EIC, p. 131)

Day 5
APPROPRIATE ALTRUISTIC CONCERN

What God's Word Says

"Do nothing out of selfish ambition or vain conceit. Rather, in humility, value others above yourselves, not looking to your interests but each of you to the interests of others. In your relationships with one another, have the same mindset as Christ Jesus:

Who, being in very nature God, did not consider equality with God something to be used to his own advantage; rather, he made himself nothing by taking the very nature of a servant, being made in human likeness. And being found in appearance as a man, he humbled himself by becoming obedient to death—even death on a cross!" **(Philippians 2:3–8)**.

Pause & Reflect

How do you feel about altruism? Look up the definition. What are the obstacles you can identify that keep you from practicing it more?

....
....
....
....
....
....

Day 5 Appropriate Altruistic Concern

A PRAYER FOR TODAY

Father, Son, and Holy Spirit,

Thank you for the ways in which you've revealed yourself to me. Thank you for the times in which I have experienced your love for me. Please let this experience spill over into my relationships and bless others too.

In Jesus's name,

Amen

Today's Topic
EGO VS. ALTRUISM: THE BATTLE IS REAL

Extra! Extra! Ego vs. Altruism—5pm! Who Will Win Today?

Every day we are navigating a myriad of choices and decisions. How will we respond to a specific person? How will we interact with others while we are in traffic? How do we carry ourselves in a specific social situation? How do we respond to an apology? Do we offer one ourselves? How do we respond to God when we sense Him nudging us?

When our ego is at the helm (remember, we used the acronym EGO: *Edging God Out*)[4], we are most concerned with ourselves. What will make us look good, what will help us get ahead, what will feel good to us, what will protect us, what will put our minds at ease? When our ego is driving our decisions, love for God and neighbor are relegated to the sidelines of our lives. And since our value system gets distorted as soon as God is not at its center, everything gets pulled out of proportion—our view of God, neighbor, and even ourselves.

Altruism, when motivated by love of God and neighbor, is a healing salve for many of our ailments. It sets things aright. It is an opportunity to put someone else's needs first (which is good for our soul), has us reaching out to our neighbors in love (which is good for our relationships), and (when we're giving sacrificially) gives us the opportunity to grow in faith (which is good for our relationship with God). It reduces our (over)focus on ourselves. All of this relegates the ego to its proper place.

As we addressed on Day 3 of this week's reflections, we don't have to be self-less to be humble. We can be self-full and freely choose to place that full, whole self in service to God and neighbor. In our experience, this is a recipe for joy. After all, we were made for this! We are part of God's ecosystem, members of a body that is made to bless and lift each other up. Our greatest joy comes in the measure through which we serve others.

Can altruism be taken advantage of? Yes. Is it still (usually) the best way to live? Yes. There is no guarantee that your loving service will be honored, appreciated, or even noticed (although we hope it will). In fact, there are times when someone becomes so unsafe, that continuing to give to them generously is no longer wise or healthy. This is where discernment is needed to keep altruism within appropriate bounds.

But generally speaking, throughout Scripture we see God honoring those who remain faithful and give to others as unto Him, even when they go unnoticed and underappreciated by their peers. Who do you know who is regularly and generously giving of themselves? Is there anything you can do to show them your appreciation? That too is altruism in action—a way to support and encourage a healthy ecosystem in the body of Christ.

Look Inside

Have you ever been the recipient of appropriate altruistic concern? How did it feel? What was it like?

Have you ever been the recipient of inappropriate altruistic concern? An unhealthy need for approval (The Drug of Approval) or overcare behavior (the Disease to Please). How did that feel? What was that like?

How would you describe God's way of giving? Can you think of 5 adjectives that describe it?

1.
2.
3.
4.
5.

What would you say makes altruism appropriate?

Altruistic Attitude/Social Awareness Week 4

Is there anyone you can think of who has given to you in such a generous and kind way that you would like to thank them? Who might that be?

_____

To Sum It Up

- ✝ Altruism is love in action.
- ✝ Our personal experience of God's love helps us love others selflessly.
- ✝ There are times when altruism is not appropriate.
- ✝ Altruism, when motivated by love of God and neighbor, is a healing salve for many of our ailments.

Meditation Moment

Please pray this adaptation of Philippians 2:3–5

Lord, I don't want to do anything for the wrong reasons. Please uproot any selfish ambition or vain conceit out of my life. Instead, please fill me with humility, that I would value others above myself, not looking only to my own interests, but considering the needs of others first. Please show me the right balance there; help me to have the same mindset as Jesus.

In Jesus's name,

Amen

Action Items

- ✝ Write this week's Bible verse out from memory on the lines below. Don't cheat! Once you have written it out and reviewed it, go back and check it with your handwritten original. How did you do?

  _____
  _____
  _____
  _____

- ✝ Build on the previous days' practices and ask God if there is anyone else in your neighborhood He would like you to meet. Walk out into your world with an eye for your neighbor and a heart open to love. If you don't meet anyone, pray for your neighborhood and ask God to bless it.

continued

Day 5 Appropriate Altruistic Concern

> ### Action Items (cont.)
> ✝ Build on the previous days' listening practices of intentionally hearing what people are saying and/or suggesting/implying. Practice listening to them from a heart of altruistic concern. If you feel the Spirit move, ask them if they would like your help.
> ✝ Build on the previous days' prayer practices of including others in your prayers. Is there anyone new you can add to your list today?

EIC = ENCOUNTER + IDENTIFIED BEHAVIOR + COURSE CORRECT

Daily EIC Reflection

Encounter (E)

Describe one Christ Encounter you had today on the lines below. What happened? Where were you? Whom did you encounter? If you're not sure which one to choose, ask the Holy Spirit to highlight one God-ordained Encounter for you.

_____
_____
_____
_____
_____
_____
_____
_____

IDENTIFIED BEHAVIOR (I)

What behaviors did you act out? Drawing on your newfound understanding in today's lesson, which of your own personality traits and motivations were at play? What were the other person's personality traits and motivations that influenced the encounter? Describe them here:

My unique personality traits and motivations:

....
....
....
....

The other person's unique personality traits and motivations:

....
....
....
....

How did these distinct traits and motivations interact with each other? Was there a clash? Did they complement each other? Reflect on this below:

....
....
....
....

COURSE CORRECT (C)

How did you respond? On a Spirit scale from 1–10, how did you do? Were you able to thoughtfully respond rather than react? Did you successfully surrender to God's will and course correct before you took action? Is there anything you wish you had done differently? Remember that we are going for *progress over perfection*. We are all here to learn and grow. Which lessons would you like to take with you going forward? What did you learn? Reflect on your answers to these questions below:

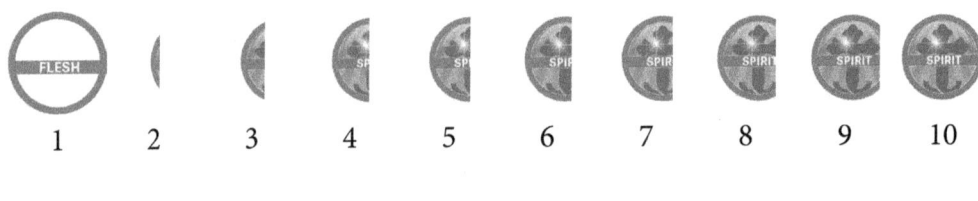

....
....

Day 5 Appropriate Altruistic Concern

Endnotes

1   https://www.snopes.com/fact-check/look-for-the-helpers/ Accessed 12/29/22. The TV Series Mr. Rogers used the phrase "Look for the helpers" when catastrophes happened. He was rtying to help children deal with emotional trauma. Rewrite original.

2   Charles Van Engen (Professor of Biblical Theology, Fuller Theological Seminary), lecture notes, September 2009.

3   This phrase refers to the process of internalizing of things we know to be true in our minds and embedding them in our hearts. More at "The Longest Journey." Accessed 12/30/2022. https://www.bluesparrowbooks.org/blogs/quote-of-the-day/the-longest-journey

4   See EIC, p. 97

Intro to Week 5
Christ Connections
(Relational Management)

Welcome Message

Welcome to Week 5, where we will focus on growing our capacity for relationship.

Relationships are such powerful motivators in our lives. Ask anyone what has made the biggest impact on them and it will likely be a relationship. This week we will look at which rules we are playing by as we engage in life and what it means to love each other (according to Jesus). One way Jesus models love for us is by being present and interruptible. We will allow ourselves to be challenged by His example. Then we will practice keeping our eyes open for divine appointments—people God might be bringing our way specifically so they might encourage us or we might encourage them. Finally, we will dwell on persevering and never giving up.

As we've said before, please engage in this process as much as possible. Just like any program or tool, you get out of it what you put into it. Allow yourself to be challenged by the questions and reflection opportunities contained here. Allow yourself to be stretched and grow. Enjoy this opportunity to intentionally set aside time for spiritual renewal.

We hope this week's study will encourage you to keep a godly perspective, be on the lookout for divine appointments throughout your day, and never give up.

Connecting Hearts in Him,

Estella, Lauren, and Rich

MEMORY VERSE FOR THE WEEK

"Love must be sincere. Hate what is evil; cling to what is good. Be devoted to one another in love. Honor one another above yourselves. Never be lacking in zeal, but keep your spiritual fervor, serving the Lord. Be joyful in hope, patient in affliction, faithful in prayer. Share with the Lord's people who are in need. Practice hospitality"
(Romans 12:9–13).

A SUPPORT RESOURCE FOR THE WEEK TO EXPLORE
Edge God In Podcast: Jesus Was Interruptible . . . Are You?
https://edgeGodin.com/edgeGo-din-podcast-week-22-Jesus-was-interruptible-are-you/

CHRIST CONNECTIONS (RELATIONAL MANAGEMENT) WEEK 5

QUOTE FOR THE DAY

"Which game are you playing? The eternal or the finite game of life? The eternal game is God-focused and other people oriented. The eternal game of life offers many opportunities for learning and growth through a variety of interruptions and pauses to create godly character for an ultimate good on earth far beyond self. The finite game is self-oriented, fast and furious, pushy, demanding, and insecure with little patience and a lot of frustration due to the inconvenience of being slowed down by interruptions. The choice is yours and what you choose will make ALL the difference in the outcomes you experience when it comes to Christ Connections." (EIC, p. 169)

"Let's pull back the curtain once again and follow the lead of our emotionally intelligent mentor Jesus Christ of Nazareth who consistently sowed to please the Spirit and as a result transformed the lives of all who were willing to believe." (EIC, p. 151)

Day 1
ARE YOU PLAYING THE ETERNAL OR FINITE GAME OF LIFE?

What God's Word Says

"A farmer went out to sow his seed. As he was scattering the seed, some fell along the path, and the birds came and ate it up. Some fell on rocky places, where it did not have much soil. It sprang up quickly, because the soil was shallow. But when the sun came up, the plants were scorched, and they withered because they had no root. Other seed fell among thorns, which grew up and choked the plants Still other seed fell on good soil, where it produced a crop—a hundred, sixty or thirty times what was sown. Whoever has ears, let them hear" **(Matthew 13:3–9).**

"Do not be deceived: God cannot be mocked. A man reaps what he sows. Whoever sows to please their flesh, from the flesh will reap destruction; whoever sows to please the Spirit, from the Spirit will reap eternal life. Let us not become weary in doing good, for at the proper time we will reap a harvest if we do not give up Therefore, as we have opportunity, let us do good to all people, especially to those who belong to the family of believers" (Galatians 6:7–10).

Pause & Reflect

How good are you at slowing down and adjusting to the needs of others in the moment? Would you say you are naturally more task or people oriented? Can you think of a time when you were able to stop what you were doing and readjust your plans based on the needs of another? Was this easy or hard for you to do?

....
....
....
....
....
....
....
....
....
....

A PRAYER FOR TODAY

God, I admit that it's easy for me to fall into a life that is self-oriented, fast and furious, pushy, demanding, and insecure. It's easy for me to put myself first. It comes naturally. I want measurable outcomes, I want success, I want to be seen and acknowledged and honored and praised. I want results and I want them now.

Please forgive me when, for all my efficiency, I miss the bigger picture, miss your vision, miss opportunities to plant seeds for eternity. Please realign my priorities with yours so I can live into your value system, your definition of success, and your timeline. Show me how to connect to people the way you did when you walked this earth: allowing God's love to lead the way even in the midst of messy emotions and undesirable behaviors.

In Jesus's name,

Amen

Today's Topic
THE CHOICE IS YOURS

The parable of the sower is a great example of someone who knows they are in it for the long haul. No farmer expects an immediate return on their investment; they know that harvesting the fruit of their labor will take time. It also encourages us to consider what kind of seed we might be. Are we passionate but short-lived in our discipleship? Burned out and disinterested? Or do we grow slowly and steadily further down into the ground and taller up into the air?

In the Psalms we encounter a lament we may all be able to relate to: Why do the wicked prosper while the righteous don't? (See Psalm 37, for example.) Another way of saying this might be: Why do the people who are only playing the finite game of life seem to be winning?

I suppose the answer to this question will have to do with our definition of success. Also, what time horizon are you considering? Does your time horizon stretch into eternity? Jesus didn't look "successful" while He was hanging on the cross and dying for our sins, but He accomplished the greatest feat mankind ever has—making a way for all of us to have a relationship with God. Had he been thinking about the immediate or short-term returns on this investment, there is no way He would have concluded that His sacrifice would pay off. But Hebrews tells us that "for the joy set before him" He went to the cross. His time horizon reached far beyond his own (human) lifetime. He had a much grander vision and a much loftier long-term (eternal) goal.

What we consider a worthy "investment" of our time, energy, and resources today has a lot to do with our time horizon. Financial advisors, for example, before they advise on investment decisions, typically want to know two important factors about us before giving us advice: (1) What is our risk tolerance? And (2) what is our time horizon?

Following God faithfully will challenge us to rethink both of these categories in light of God's power and in light of eternity. What is your time horizon for your return on investment? If you need to see a return on your investment of love, care, and concern today (or even in this lifetime), you might grow discouraged, despair, and not last long in your discipleship walk. To return to the Parable of the Sower, you might be a seed that dies, gives up, and loses interest. But if you accept the fact that some of your investments may not yield a return until you reach heaven and can manage to trust God with the outcome now, it will be easier for you to align your actions ("investments") with His eternal objectives and beautiful long-term (eternal) goals.

Letting go of the immediate outcomes of our faithfulness is hard to do. We come face-to-face with our desire for control, approval, and recognition. But what is better? A pat on the back now or a "well done, good and faithful servant"[1] then? The choice is yours. As Mother Teresa said: "God didn't call me to be successful, He called me to be faithful."

Look Inside

How easy is it for you to delay gratification/wait for a positive outcome?
- ✟ Easy peasy. God's in control.
- ✟ Depends on the day.
- ✟ To be honest, it's tough.
- ✟ It's driving me crazy!

When you're making decisions, do you typically take the eternal repercussions into consideration? If you did so more often, how would that change the way you went about making decisions?

What percentage of the time would you say you're currently playing the finite game? What percentage of the time do you manage to play by eternal values?

Are there certain triggers that instantly distract you from God's eternal standards and tempt you to play the finite game of life (by responding to others in a way that is short-lived and driven by strong negative emotions)? If you're not sure what they are, take some time to ask the Holy Spirit about them now. What is He showing you?

Now that God has revealed some of these triggers to you, what would you like to do about them?

Christ Connections (Relational Management) Week 5

....
....

Talk to God about them now.

To Sum It Up

- ✞ Are you playing the eternal or finite game of life? The choice is yours.
- ✞ Following Jesus challenges us to reassess our priorities in light of eternal values.
- ✞ Sometimes following God faithfully means delaying gratification/reward and expanding our time horizons for our return on investment—even into the next life.
- ✞ Jesus is our living example of someone who faithfully lived and lives by eternal values (even unto death) and is therefore reaping eternal rewards.

Meditation Moment

Today, let's reflect on goodness. What does it feel like, look like, act like, talk like, walk like? Where are you seeing goodness in the world right now? Who do you know who is spreading goodness? How can you contribute to the overall goodness in the world today?

Action Items

- ✞ Read this week's memory verse (along with the reference where it can be found) three times and manually write it out here:

  _____
  _____
  _____
  _____

- ✞ Is there a financial need you're aware of that you can assist with? Prayerfully consider being the answer to someone's prayer.
- ✞ Is there a child you're aware of in need of tutoring, mentoring, babysitting, or coaching? Prayerfully consider filling that need.
- ✞ Is there a food bank you're aware of in need of supplies? Prayerfully consider feeding someone today by contributing to it anonymously.
- ✞ Is there a lonely person you're aware of who's in need of a cup of coffee and a visit? Prayerfully consider making that person's day.

Do any (or all) of these things not to help or fix anyone, but to simply spread some goodness around. No other agenda or outcome necessary simply be aware of the opportunities to make Jesus recognizable in someone's life today.

EIC = ENCOUNTER + IDENTIFIED BEHAVIOR + COURSE CORRECT

Daily EIC Reflection

ENCOUNTER (E)

Describe one Christ Encounter you had today on the lines below. What happened? Where were you? Whom did you encounter? If you're not sure which one to choose, ask the Holy Spirit to highlight one God-ordained Encounter for you.

IDENTIFIED BEHAVIOR (I)

What behaviors did you act out? Drawing on your newfound understanding in today's lesson, which of your own personality traits and motivations were at play? What were the other person's personality traits and motivations that influenced the encounter? Describe them here:

My unique personality traits and motivations:

The other person's unique personality traits and motivations:

How did these distinct traits and motivations interact with each other? Was there a clash? Did they complement each other? Reflect on this below:

COURSE CORRECT (C)

How did you respond? On a Spirit scale from 1–10, how did you do? Were you able to thoughtfully respond rather than react? Did you successfully surrender to God's will and course correct before you took action? Is there anything you wish you had done differently? Remember that we are going for *progress over perfection*. We are all here to learn and grow. Which lessons would you like to take with you going forward? What did you learn? Reflect on your answers to these questions below:

QUOTE FOR THE DAY

"Jesus's love evokes more love." (EIC, p. 149)

"How you handle the emotions of other people in the midst of your connection is a game changer when it comes to your ability to manage the gifts and talents of people entrusted to your care." (EIC, p. 146)

"We can't love other people without first encountering God's love for us through Christ (1 John 4:19) [. . .] We can't make an authentic positive connection (void of selfish ambition and false motives) in relationships with other people unless we are personally connected to Christ within us." (EIC, p. 145)

Day 2
LOVING ONE ANOTHER

What God's Word Says

"A new command I give you: Love one another. As I have loved you, so you must love one another. By this, everyone will know that you are my disciples if you love one another" **(John 13:34–35)**.

"Our own body has many parts. When all these many parts are put together, they are only one body. The body of Christ is like this. It is the same way with us. Jews or those who are not Jews, men who are owned by someone or men who are free to do what they want to do, have all been baptized into the one body by the same Holy Spirit. We have all received the one Spirit" **(1 Corinthians 12:13)**.

Pause & Reflect

How much of your time do you spend thinking about loving other people well? How much of your time do you spend thinking about being loved?

....
....
....
....
....
....

A PRAYER FOR TODAY

Loving God, I am aware that I do not always love well. I have not loved you with my whole heart and I have not loved my neighbor as myself. I am truly sorry and I humbly repent.

For the sake of your Son Jesus Christ, have mercy on me and forgive me; that I may delight in your will, and walk in your ways, to the glory of your Name.[2]

Where I have failed to love others well, God, please bring it to my attention so I may go and seek reconciliation. Where I have failed to love you well, God, please show me this as well so I may confess it and start afresh. And where I have failed to love myself well, God, please forgive me and grant me increased capacity to love everyone, including myself.

Holy Spirit, Lord and Giver of Life, please increase my capacity to both give and receive your love generously.

In Jesus's name,

Amen

Today's Topic
BEING A FAITHFUL MANAGER OF GIFTS

In Matthew 25:14–30 we read a parable Jesus tells about bags of gold, also known as talents, a rich man entrusts to his servants. What if we applied that story of stewardship to our relationships with other people? In this case, the quality of our relationships could be compared to the talents entrusted to the servants. We have several options as to how to handle their various personality types and traits that may or may not naturally pair easily with our own.

We can stick our heads in the sand, bury these talents, not confront/address/recognize our differences, and not ask the Holy Spirit to give us creative tools to reach one another, making sure no growth occurs. This may seem "safe" in terms of preserving the status quo, but it doesn't grow the relationship with the people entrusted to our care. If fear is present (fear of rejection, loss of power, criticism or loss of routine) it doesn't allow us to really see and love people because we are in a protection mode. Worst of all, it doesn't encourage an authentic Christ Connection; it doesn't encourage those entrusted to our care to grow. The response to this choice can be seen in Matthew 25:26: The rich man is not pleased.

We are in the driver's seat of the choices we make when it comes to our focus, attention and time. We can choose to invest some time and emotional energy into understanding and caring for the people God has brought into our lives. We can bring a degree of intentionality into these encounters. We can cover them with prayer. We can ask the Holy Spirit to help us see and hear each other. Even a limited or cursory interest in growing our own emotional intelligence in Christ will certainly yield some fruit. There will be growth (both in us and in others), there will be fruit for the kingdom, and just as in our text in Matthew 25:23, the rich man will be pleased.

Best of all, we can go all in on understanding and growing our capacities for emotional intelligence and loving people well. We can work on stopping our automatic assumptions and inferences (see EIC, p. 161) and practice responding in top-down ways rather than from the bottom up. We can become less reactionary and defensive and more curious, able to delay our natural trigger-happy responses in order to more authentically encounter "the other." There is no doubt developing these (admittedly challenging) skills requires real effort but the outcome can be seen in Matthew 25:21 of our text: Though the effort may be significant, it will not be in vain.

Look Inside

How eager are you to invest in relationships? Is this a joyful task for you or do you consider it more of a chore?

- ✞ Oh yes, it's natural!
- ✞ Depends on the day.
- ✞ To be honest, they are a lot of work. Relationships exhaust me.
- ✞ They scare me to death.
- ✞ They are impossible! No matter what I do, I can't win.

Have you ever invested in relationships and been hurt? What happened?

Can you recall a time when you invested in relationships and were overwhelmed by the (positive) response? What was that like?

Overall, would you say the investment we make in relationships is worth it or not?

- ✞ Yes, absolutely.
- ✞ It depends.
- ✞ Honestly, I'm not sure.
- ✞ Based on my experience, I'd have to say no.

Of all the people you know personally (excluding Jesus), who is excellent at loving others and nurturing wholesome relationships? What is it about them that makes them so good at what they do?

To Sum It Up

✝ Jesus commands us to love one another (John 13:34–35)
✝ Although relationships take some intentionality, our efforts will not (forever) be in vain.
✝ Encountering God's love for us helps us love other people well.

Meditation Moment

Let's pray:

God, I want to be a gamechanger for somebody today. When their emotions come at me and I feel unprepared, please give me the grace to see them, hear them, and love them well. I know it matters to you how we love others; please grow my capacity to love.

In Jesus's name,

Amen

Action Items

✝ Read this week's memory verse out loud three times, each time trying to commit more of it to memory. Think about what it means and why each of the words were chosen when it was originally written. Create any memory aids you can think of. Rather than read it in print, read your own handwritten version (from yesterday) to help you memorize it.
✝ The next time you hit the limits of your capacity to love well, breathe, stop, and ask God to increase your capacity. Then receive it.
✝ Watch and listen to "Christ Has No Body Now but Yours"[9] on YouTube.
✝ Write God a poem, expressing how you feel about Him.

EIC = ENCOUNTER + IDENTIFIED BEHAVIOR + COURSE CORRECT

Daily EIC Reflection

ENCOUNTER (E)

Describe one Christ Encounter you had today on the lines below. What happened? Where were you? Whom did you encounter? If you're not sure which one to choose, ask the Holy Spirit to highlight one God-ordained Encounter for you.

IDENTIFIED BEHAVIOR (I)

What behaviors did you act out? Drawing on your newfound understanding in today's lesson, which of your own personality traits and motivations were at play? What were the other person's personality traits and motivations that influenced the encounter? Describe them here:

My unique personality traits and motivations:

The other person's unique personality traits and motivations:

How did these distinct traits and motivations interact with each other? Was there a clash? Did they complement each other? Reflect on this below:

COURSE CORRECT (C)

How did you respond? On a Spirit scale from 1–10, how did you do? Were you able to thoughtfully respond rather than react? Did you successfully surrender to God's will and course correct before you took action? Is there anything you wish you had done differently? Remember that we are going for *progress over perfection*. We are all here to learn and grow. Which lessons would you like to take with you going forward? What did you learn? Reflect on your answers to these questions below:

1 2 3 4 5 6 7 8 9 10

QUOTE FOR THE DAY

"Jesus did one consistent emotionally intelligent behavior that is worth our attention in the midst of a hurried culture: He allowed himself to be interrupted for the sake of healing, restoring, and loving people. The result? He created connections that transformed lives forever." (EIC, p. 151)

"They didn't have to change to encounter Jesus's love and forgiveness. Jesus's love and forgiveness positively changed them and their ability to connect with people." (EIC, p. 149)

"Dear Lord, [. . .] Interrupt me when I think I am my struggle and remind me of my identity and purpose in and through you." (EIC, p. 152)

"Are you interruptible for Christ Connections in the midst of the hustle for God's love, healing, and restoration to step into the lives of the people around you?" (EIC, p. 153)

DAY 3
BEING PRESENT & INTERRUPTIBLE

What God's Word Says

"We are therefore Christ's ambassadors, as though God were making his appeal through us. We implore you on Christ's behalf: Be reconciled to God" **(2 Corinthians 5:20).**

"Do not conform to the pattern of this world, but be transformed by the renewing of your mind. Then you will be able to test and approve what God's will is—his good, pleasing and perfect will" **(Romans 12:2).**

"People were also bringing babies to Jesus for him to place his hands on them. When the disciples saw this, they rebuked them. But Jesus called the children to him and said, 'Let the little children come to me, and do not hinder them, for the kingdom of God belongs to such as these. Truly I tell you, anyone who will not receive the kingdom of God like a little child will never enter it" **(Luke 18:15–17).**

Pause & Reflect

How interruptible are you? Do you enjoy interruptions and go with the flow or are they irritating to you?

A PRAYER FOR TODAY

"Dear Lord, move me into the kind of faith that the centurion soldier had. I want to fill You with wonder today because of my choice to pause, believe, and take action grounded in faith for the good of the people You entrusted to my care." (EIC, p. 155)

In Jesus's name,

Amen

Today's Topic
THE ABILITY TO CONNECT

Because truly connecting with people requires energy and commitment, some of us try our best to avoid it. Like a WIFI router that keeps dropping the signal, a person who is unable or unwilling to connect causes frustration and sometimes pain. How many of us have tried to connect with someone over time who is simply unable or unwilling to receive us? Few things are as hurtful and few things cause as much emotional harm.

How healing and restorative, then, to encounter someone who can receive us, hear us, and truly connect with us.

As sad as it may be, in the global West true connection is rare. Isolation and loneliness are killing people and mental health crises are on the rise. Recently the COVID-19 pandemic really highlighted the fragility of our networks and our communities. For some people who were already employed and well connected, it posed some challenges but wasn't devastating. For others, who were already feeling economically challenged, isolated, and lonely before the pandemic hit, it presented overwhelming trauma.

Supposedly being alone is one of our greatest human fears. We stay in abusive marriages, go along with peer pressure, and give in to other people's expectations of us, all because we fear rejection, shunning, and isolation. How many of us have done something we regret for fear of standing alone? Our desire to belong is a powerful motivator.

What does it do for us, then, to be accepted *just as we are*? To be both truly seen AND loved? Well, to restate the first quote in The Quote of the Day above: It changes our lives forever.

Look Inside

Recall a time when someone received you, heard you, and truly connected with you. How did that make you feel?

What was it about their behavior that made such a big impact?

_____
_____
_____
_____

Who are the people in your life that you're allowed to call/text/interrupt at any time?

_____
_____
_____
_____

How do you know that that's the case? What is it about them that lets you know you are welcome in their lives?

_____
_____
_____
_____

Do you believe that Jesus is eager, excited even, to be interrupted by you?
- ✞ Oh yes, that's who He is! He loves hearing from me!
- ✞ Umm, I'm not so sure.
- ✞ Maybe, if I'm good enough.
- ✞ I don't think so.

Is there anything you'd like to tell him?

_____
_____
_____
_____

To Sum It Up

† Jesus models for us a consistent lifestyle of being present and interruptible.
† Being interruptible shows people that they are important, even a priority.
† Sometimes being interruptible can make a life-changing impact.
† Connecting with others deeply helps alleviate some of our greatest fears.

Meditation Moment

Today let's reflect on this sentence:

"He allowed himself to be interrupted for the sake of healing, restoring, and loving people."

In the space below, prayerfully write the following sentence by hand three times:

I allow myself to be interrupted for the sake of healing, restoring, and loving people to the Glory of God.

Then let it sink in.

....
....
....
....
....

> ### Action Items
> † Record this week's memory verse on your phone (any voice recording app will do) in your own voice and listen to it three times throughout your day. Speak slowly as you record. As you listen to the recording, try following along with your own recorded voice.
> † Take out some art supplies. It can be as simple as a pen and paper or a full canvas and paints. What does "He allowed himself to be interrupted for the sake of healing, restoring, and loving people." Look like? Meditate on this as you paint/draw/sketch. What you create can be as concrete or abstract as you like.
> † The next time someone interrupts you, return to this image you painted in your mind. Access what you were feeling when you created this artwork. Access what you learned. Bring that same reverence into the space with the person who is interrupting you.

Christ Connections (Relational Management) Week 5

EIC = ENCOUNTER + IDENTIFIED BEHAVIOR + COURSE CORRECT

Daily EIC Reflection

ENCOUNTER (E)

Describe one Christ Encounter you had today on the lines below. What happened? Where were you? Whom did you encounter? If you're not sure which one to choose, ask the Holy Spirit to highlight one God-ordained Encounter for you.

....
....
....
....
....
....
....
....

IDENTIFIED BEHAVIOR (I)

What behaviors did you act out? Drawing on your newfound understanding in today's lesson, which of your own personality traits and motivations were at play? What were the other person's personality traits and motivations that influenced the encounter? Describe them here:

My unique personality traits and motivations:

....
....
....
....

The other person's unique personality traits and motivations:

....
....
....
....

How did these distinct traits and motivations interact with each other? Was there a clash? Did they complement each other? Reflect on this below:

....
....
....
....

COURSE CORRECT (C)

How did you respond? On a Spirit scale from 1–10, how did you do? Were you able to thoughtfully respond rather than react? Did you successfully surrender to God's will and course correct before you took action? Is there anything you wish you had done differently? Remember that we are going for *progress over perfection*. We are all here to learn and grow. Which lessons would you like to take with you going forward? What did you learn? Reflect on your answers to these questions below:

| 1 | 2 | 3 | 4 | 5 | 6 | 7 | 8 | 9 | 10 |

....
....
....
....
....
....
....
....

QUOTE FOR THE DAY

"People before things leads to things that champion people." (EIC, p. 156)

"Invite the Holy Spirit to bump you out of selfish ambition and toss you into selflessness that will produce a harvest more than eye can see or ear can hear." (EIC, p. 155)

"Love pauses. Love notices those in need. Love seeks out an opportunity to edify and encourage. Love puts the needs of another before its own. Love allows itself to be interrupted for a greater good than the task at hand. Love returns 10-fold, abundant joy and peace to those who allow themselves to be interrupted for the sake of more love in the world." (EIC, p. 152)

DAY 4
LOOKING FOR DIVINE APPOINTMENTS

What God's Word Says

Now an angel of the Lord said to Philip, "Go south to the road—the desert road—that goes down from Jerusalem to Gaza." So he started out, and on his way he met an Ethiopian eunuch, an important official in charge of all the treasury of the Kandake (which means "queen of the Ethiopians"). This man had gone to Jerusalem to worship, and on his way home was sitting in his chariot reading the Book of Isaiah the prophet. The Spirit told Philip, "Go to that chariot and stay near it."

Then Philip ran up to the chariot and heard the man reading Isaiah the prophet. "Do you understand what you are reading?" Philip asked.

"How can I," he said, "unless someone explains it to me?" So he invited Philip to come up and sit with him."

This is the passage of Scripture the eunuch was reading:

> He was led like a sheep to the slaughter,
>   and as a lamb before its shearer is silent,
>   so he did not open his mouth.
> In his humiliation he was deprived of justice.
>   Who can speak of his descendants?

Day 4 Looking for Divine Appointments

> For his life was taken from the earth.
>
> The eunuch asked Philip, "Tell me, please, who is the prophet talking about, himself or someone else?" Then Philip began with that very passage of Scripture and told him the good news about Jesus.
>
> As they traveled along the road, they came to some water and the eunuch said, "Look, here is water. What can stand in the way of my being baptized?" And he gave orders to stop the chariot. Then both Philip and the eunuch went down into the water and Philip baptized him. When they came up out of the water, the Spirit of the Lord suddenly took Philip away, and the eunuch did not see him again, but went on his way rejoicing. Philip, however, appeared at Azotus and traveled about, preaching the gospel in all the towns until he reached Caesarea.
>
> (As told in Acts 8:26–40.)

Pause & Reflect

Are you used to looking for divine appointments throughout your day? Is this a practice you have honed or is this practice new to you?

_____
_____
_____
_____
_____
_____
_____
_____
_____
_____

A PRAYER FOR TODAY

Lord, I want to be aware of you today. I want to be aware of your Spirit. I want to go into my day with eager expectation that you'll show up and do something amazing. I want to be tuned in to what you are doing; I don't want to miss it. When you move, I want to be ready.

Please help me to pay attention to you. Please help me to be in touch with your heart. Please help me to notice, cherish, and appreciate the divine appointments you bring my way today, even if they feel like interruptions. Please give me grace for each person I interact with today.

In Jesus's name,

Amen

Day 4 Looking for Divine Appointments

Today's Topic
Spectacles for the Spectacular

In a previous reflection, on Day 3 of Week 1, we entitled our topic, "The Goggles of God" and addressed the way God sees us. Today's reflection is about seeing too but instead of focusing on how God sees us, today's reflection is on what spectacles we put on before stepping out into our day. Do we step out with low expectations of God (or even give him a second thought) and take a frenzied, haphazard approach to our day with a sense of always running behind or do we go into our day with eyes of faith and wonder, eagerly expecting God to show up and do something amazing in our relationships?

One such amazing thing God might do in our day is orchestrate a divine appointment. It may happen at the grocery store, in the boardroom, at the bus station, or in your boss's office. It may be with someone you've known for years or with a complete stranger. It may be obvious to you in the moment or you may only realize it days or even years later. The question is: Are you ready?

To put on our special Spectacles for the Spectacular requires inner preparation; we must be intentional. We may already be aware of the Bible's admonition to put on the full armor of God (Ephesians 6), but aren't we forgetting this quintessential accessory? When we know who God is, what he has done for us, and what his heart is for the world, we can go out into his beloved world with a sense of anticipation. This, too, is faith. Rather than randomly stumbling through our day, we can be actively looking for God to show up. We can anticipate his goodness by faith. We can pray and ask for divine appointments. We can request that God lead us into the right conversations with the right people at the right time. We can ready our heart to love. We can ready our spirit (and our feet) with the gospel of peace.

In 2 Timothy 4:2 we are admonished to be prepared in season and out of season. The difference between the bridesmaids with the lamps who caught the bridegroom and the ones who didn't was preparation (see Matthew 25). Are you prepared for grandeur? Are you prepared for majesty? Are you prepared for a miracle to happen today?

After all, we worship a mighty, majestic, miraculous God. Why wouldn't he do something magnificent? Come on, grab those spectacles and let's go!

Look Inside

How often do you step out into your day, expecting God to show up and send a divine appointment your way?

- ✞ All the time!
- ✞ Sometimes.
- ✞ Every once in a while.
- ✞ I never even thought to do so!

Can you think of an encounter you've had that you would consider a divine appointment, now that you're looking back? How did that go? What made it so special?

_____
_____
_____
_____
_____

Do you think you've ever been a divine appointment in someone else's day? If so, can you describe that memory?

_____
_____
_____
_____
_____

What do you think might make you available or tuned in to divine appointments? Is there anything you can do to make them happen more often?

_____
_____
_____
_____
_____

Day 4 Looking for Divine Appointments

What kind of habits, behaviors, or mindsets do you associate with wearing "spectacles for the spectacular"? How many of them can you think of?

To Sum It Up

- ✢ What we might perceive as surprises or interruptions might actually be divine appointments.
- ✢ We can ready ourselves for these by leaning in to who God is and by expecting great things from Him.
- ✢ Love pauses.
- ✢ Divine appointments are a great opportunity to practice love in our everyday lives.

Meditation Moment

"Love pauses." Let's dwell on this for a moment.

Take a moment to calm your body and take three deep, slow breaths. Try to make them slower and deeper each time, breathing out all the way.

Now pay attention to the pause between your inhale and your exhale. As you repeat this exercise, think about the power of the pause to change your behavior and change someone else's day, week, or even life.

Action Items

- ✢ Listen to your recording of this week's Bible verse again. Now try reciting it from memory (without the recording). Can you do it? Don't forget to quote the reference. Keep practicing it until you feel confident.
- ✢ Make it a game: Invite the Holy Spirit to bump you out of selfish ambition and toss you into selflessness. See what happens!
- ✢ Interrupt your irritation with gratitude: The next time someone interrupts you, thank God for bringing someone your way to love.
- ✢ Keep an eye out for divine appointments. For we are Christ's ambassadors and He is making His appeal through us every day. **(2 Corinthians 5:20)**

EIC = ENCOUNTER + IDENTIFIED BEHAVIOR + COURSE CORRECT

Daily EIC Reflection

ENCOUNTER (E)

Describe one Christ Encounter you had today on the lines below. What happened? Where were you? Whom did you encounter? If you're not sure which one to choose, ask the Holy Spirit to highlight one God-ordained Encounter for you.

IDENTIFIED BEHAVIOR (I)

What behaviors did you act out? Drawing on your newfound understanding in today's lesson, which of your own personality traits and motivations were at play? What were the other person's personality traits and motivations that influenced the encounter? Describe them here.

My unique personality traits and motivations:

The other person's unique personality traits and motivations:

Day 4 Looking for Divine Appointments

How did these distinct traits and motivations interact with each other? Was there a clash? Did they complement each other? Reflect on this below:

COURSE CORRECT (C)

How did you respond? On a Spirit scale from 1–10, how did you do? Were you able to thoughtfully respond rather than react? Did you successfully surrender to God's will and course correct before you took action? Is there anything you wish you had done differently? Remember that we are going for *progress over perfection*. We are all here to learn and grow. Which lessons would you like to take with you going forward? What did you learn? Reflect on your answers to these questions below:

1 2 3 4 5 6 7 8 9 10

QUOTE FOR THE DAY

"In order to create intentional Christ Connections, our ability to remain in Christ (John 15) is essential. Without Christ within us, there are too many triggers that hijack our ability to connect." (EIC, p. 164)

Day 5
PERSEVERING: DO NOT GIVE UP!

What God's Word Says

"Do not be deceived: God cannot be mocked. A man reaps what he sows. Whoever sows to please their flesh, from the flesh will reap destruction; whoever sows to please the Spirit, from the Spirit will reap eternal life. Let us not become weary in doing good, for at the proper time we will reap a harvest if we do not give up" **(Galatians 6:7–9).**

"Because of the increase of wickedness, the love of most will grow cold, but the one who stands firm to the end will be saved" **(Matthew 24:12–13).**

Not that I have already obtained all this, or have already arrived at my goal, but I press on to take hold of that for which Christ Jesus took hold of me. Brothers and sisters, I do not consider myself yet to have taken hold of it. But one thing I do: Forgetting what is behind and straining toward what is ahead, I press on toward the goal to win the prize for which God has called me heavenward in Christ Jesus" **(Philippians 3:12–14).**

"Therefore, since we are surrounded by such a great cloud of witnesses, let us throw off everything that hinders and the sin that so easily entangles. And let us run with perseverance the race marked out for us, fixing our eyes on Jesus, the pioneer and perfecter of faith" **(Hebrews 12:1–2).**

Pause & Reflect

As you reflect on running the race with perseverance, how prone are you (naturally speaking) to giving up? How prone are you to persevering? Give an example or a time when you persevered or gave up when it comes to your relationships with others.

A PRAYER FOR TODAY

Lord God, sometimes I grow weary in doing good and want to give up. People don't appreciate my efforts. I suffer disappointments and get hurt. I experience losses and wonder if continuing to follow your way is worth it. I forget the amazing ways you've come through for me in the past and get bogged down by the present.

Please help me to endure until the "proper time." Please help me to persevere. After all we've been through, I don't want to give up before the harvest time. Please help me to be faithful, hopeful, and patient. And sustain me with your joy all along the way. Thank you for your provision, Lord. With your help, I will persevere until the end and finish strong.

In Jesus's name,

Amen

Day 5 Persevering: Do Not Give Up!

Today's Topic
THE HARDEST PART

Some say that getting started is the hardest part. And certainly they have a point. It takes a tremendous amount of energy, creativity, and effort to get a new organization, hobby, vision, or relationship off the ground. But staying the course is hard too—just a different kind of hard. It requires a different skillset to persevere and stick with something for the long haul.

It's like asking runners which is harder: to sprint or to run a marathon? The truth is they are both hard. Just a different kind of hard.

When we first come to Christ, we have a lot to learn: How to trust, how to obey, who God is, what He asks of us, how to study the Bible, how to have a relationship with God, how to trust the Holy Spirit, who to trust to disciple us, how to find our way into spiritual community, etc. But later, when we've been staying the course for a while, we face new challenges: How to stay faithful in the face of disappointment, for example, how to deal with betrayal from fellow believers, or how to deal with prayer requests that remain "unanswered" for decades. When our efforts don't yield the outcomes we longed and hoped for (or even expected), and we come face-to-face with the limitations of our own power and faith, we can be prone to lose heart, disengage, and give up.

Not a small number of people give up on God after a while, when he stops "working" for them. When prayer requests go "unanswered" or they suffer grave loss and grief and don't receive the emotional and spiritual support they need. Or they see hypocrisy in fellow believers that leaves them feeling disillusioned, alienated, and alone. Resentment is a real killer. We've been told that the first indicator that members of AA (Alcoholics Anonymous) will relapse into active alcoholism is no longer faithfully attending meetings; the second is harboring resentment.

Unforgiveness, bitterness, anger, and resentment are some of the things that will suck the life and joy right out of us. So, what will it take to run the race, persevere until the end, and finish strong? Confessing our sins to God and one another is one of those things that is cleansing; it's good for the soul. It relieves some of the burdens of the sins we've accumulated; it makes our walk lighter and less lonely. It lets the light shine into some of the darker places we've been.

Another is joy. Joy is a tremendous help when it comes to perseverance. Paul, who faithfully persevered through a seemingly endless number of trials exhorts us to "Rejoice in the Lord always!"[4] Always? Always. Joy is a choice and we can choose it in obedience.

Finally, the Christian ecosystem we addressed on Day 4 of the previous week is a tremendous lifeline when it comes to persevering, remaining faithful, and not giving up. In our church communities we can find endless inspiration and encouragement: Whether it be from more experienced believers who have remained faithful for much longer than we have or from younger believers who are brimming with newly discovered excitement and enthusiasm over God's love for them, other believers can inspire and encourage us, just by being who and where they are. Hearing their God-stories can help us remember what God is like and what He has done in our lives, too, even if we are not experiencing Him in that way right now. They can pray for us, cheer us on, believe for us, and remind us of all the ways God has been faithful.

You may have heard of this wise African proverb[5]: *If you want to go fast, go alone. But if you want to go far, go together.* Let's help each other to persevere!

LOOK INSIDE

Do you consider yourself more of a loner or would you rather "go it together"? What is your personal preference? Why do you think that is the case?

....
....
....
....

When you reflect on times when you've persevered through hardship in relationship to others, what were some of the top ingredients that encouraged you and helped you go on? List 5 of them here:

1. ....
2. ....
3. ....
4. ....
5. ....

When you recall times when you gave up on something in relationship, what was it that discouraged you to the point of throwing in the towel?

....
....
....
....

Recall one time when you persevered through something really challenging in a relationship and did not give up. What were the details? Write your story down here:

To Sum It Up

- ✝ At the proper time we will reap a harvest if we do not give up. (Galatians 6:9)
- ✝ It's easier to persevere when you're not going it alone.
- ✝ Joy is a choice.
- ✝ It's worth it to persevere in doing good.

Meditation Moment

Please pray this adaptation of Hebrews 12:1–2.

Lord, thank you that you do surround me with such a great cloud of witnesses who have gone before me and have persevered faithfully. Please give me the power to throw off everything that hinders and any sin that entangles me and let me run with perseverance the race that you have marked out for me. I want to fix my eyes on you, Jesus. You are the pioneer and perfector of my faith. Thank you for clearing the way for me.

In Jesus's name,

Amen

Christ Connections (Relational Management) Week 5

Action Items

✝ Write this week's Bible verse out from memory on the lines below. Don't cheat! Once you have written it out and reviewed it, go back and check it with your handwritten original. How did you do?

_____
_____
_____
_____

✝ If you don't already have one, ask God to bring an encouragement buddy/accountability partner/prayer partner into your life. It's so much better than going it alone. If you already have one, thank God for them and be sure to meet up with them!

✝ Decide today to choose joy and love in your relationships. Simply because the Bible says so. See what happens!

✝ Draw a timeline of your life and ask the Holy Spirit to highlight for you where you have already demonstrated perseverance when it comes to relating to others as Jesus did. Ask God to help you carry on and finish strong.

EIC = ENCOUNTER + IDENTIFIED BEHAVIOR + COURSE CORRECT

Daily EIC Reflection

ENCOUNTER (E)

Describe one Christ Encounter you had today on the lines below. What happened? Where were you? Whom did you encounter? If you're not sure which one to choose, ask the Holy Spirit to highlight one God-ordained Encounter for you.

_____
_____
_____
_____
_____
_____
_____

IDENTIFIED BEHAVIOR (I)

What behaviors did you act out? Drawing on your newfound understanding in today's lesson, which of your own personality traits and motivations were at play? What were the other person's personality traits and motivations that influenced the encounter? Describe them here:

My unique personality traits and motivations:

The other person's unique personality traits and motivations:

How did these distinct traits and motivations interact with each other? Was there a clash? Did they complement each other? Reflect on this below:

COURSE CORRECT (C)

How did you respond? On a Spirit scale from 1–10, how did you do? Were you able to thoughtfully respond rather than react? Did you successfully surrender to God's will and course correct before you took action? Is there anything you wish you had done differently? Remember that we are going for *progress over perfection*. We are all here to learn and grow. Which lessons would you like to take with you going forward? What did you learn? Reflect on your answers to these questions below:

Endnotes

1 See Matthew 25:23

2 This is an adaptation of a prayer from the Book of Common Prayer. More on this resource at "Old Truths for the New Year." Accessed 12/30/2022. https://wearefaith.org/blog/old-truths-for-the-new-year-prayer-of-confession-from-book-of-common-prayer/.

3 "Christ Has No Body Now but Yours." Accessed 12/29/2022. https://www.youtube.com/watch?v=w7ymxW3rndk.

4 See Philippians 4:4.

5 "If You Want to Go Fast." Accessed 12/30/2022. https://blog.unmc.edu/publichealth/2016/09/08/if-you-want-to-go-fast-go-alone-if-you-want-to-go-far-go-together-african-proverb-martha-goedert/.

MEMORY VERSES OF THE PAST 5 WEEKS:

Week 1: *"I have been crucified with Christ and I no longer live, but Christ lives in me. The life I now live in the body, I live by faith in the Son of God, who loved me and gave himself for me"* (Galatians 2:20).

Week 2: *"But you are a chosen people, a royal priesthood, a holy nation, God's special possession, that you may declare the praises of him who called you out of darkness into his wonderful light"* (1 Peter 2:9).

Week 3: *"Remain in me, as I also remain in you. No branch can bear fruit by itself; it must remain in the vine. Neither can you bear fruit unless you remain in me. I am the vine; you are the branches. If you remain in me and I in you, you will bear much fruit; apart from me you can do nothing"* (John 15:4–5).

Week 4: *"You call me 'Teacher' and 'Lord,' and rightly so, for that is what I am. Now that I, your Lord and Teacher, have washed your feet, you also should wash one another's feet. I have set you an example that you should do as I have done for you"* (John 13:13–15).

Week 5: *"Love must be sincere. Hate what is evil; cling to what is good. Be devoted to one another in love. Honor one another above yourselves. Never be lacking in zeal, but keep your spiritual fervor, serving the Lord. Be joyful in hope, patient in affliction, faithful in prayer. Share with the Lord's people who are in need. Practice hospitality"* (Romans 12:9–13).

Intro to Week 6
Review & Reflect

Welcome Message

Welcome to Week 6, where we will take some time to intentionally look back and reflect on all we have learned!

This week's reflections will look very different from the studies of the previous weeks. Rather than give you lots of activities to do this week, we would like to encourage you to process and reflect on all you have learned. This is your time to review your Emotional Intelligence in Christ journey and allow all of your learnings to sink in and take root. It is your opportunity to synthesize the various Scripture passages, reflections, and applications you have read about, written out, prayed about, talked about, and practiced and prayerfully decide which ones of them you will incorporate into your daily life moving forward.

How has this study changed you? We would love to hear! Visit us at **EmotionalintelligenceinChrist.com**.

We applaud you for engaging in these rigorous spiritual reflections and exercises and hope it has been an enriching time of personal and spiritual growth for you. May God bless your ongoing learning, healing, and growth as you go out to love and bless the world in Jesus's name!

Connecting Hearts in Him,

Estella, Lauren, and Rich

REVIEW & REFLECT WEEK 6

Day 1
LOOK INSIDE

REVIEW:

Take some time to prayerfully review all of the *Look Inside* exercises you have done over the course of the last five weeks.

REFLECT:

As you reread your responses, what do you notice? Are there any patterns that stand out to you?

What have you learned about yourself?

What parts of your personality would you like to thank God for today?

What parts of your personality would you like to invite the Holy Spirit to transform into Christ's likeness?

Is there any behavior you would like to intentionally lay down and surrender in exchange for increased health and holiness? If so, tell God about this now:

Are there any behaviors you would like to intentionally commit to, going forward? If so, tell God about these now:

Day 2
CHRIST ENCOUNTERS

REVIEW:

Take some time to prayerfully review all of the *Christ Encounters* you experienced and journaled about over the course of the last five weeks.

REFLECT:

As you reread your reflections, what do you notice about your personality style?

_____
_____
_____
_____
_____

What have you learned about yourself?

_____
_____
_____
_____
_____
_____

What have you learned about the personalities of the people you have encountered over the course of the last five weeks?

_____
_____
_____
_____
_____
_____
_____

Are there certain personalities that are particularly challenging for you to engage with? Why do you think that is? Reflect on this here:

Are there certain personalities that are particularly fun or easy for you to engage with? Why do you think that is? Reflect on this here:

Are there any behaviors you would like to intentionally lay down and surrender in exchange for increased health and holiness? If so, tell God about and ask Him for His help with this now:

Are there any behaviors you would like to intentionally commit to, going forward? If so, tell God about these and ask Him for His help with this now:

Day 3
ACTION ITEMS

REVIEW:

Take some time to prayerfully review all of the *Action Items* over the course of the last five weeks.

REFLECT:

As you reread these, which ones stand out to you?

....
....
....
....

Which action steps were particularly helpful to you? Why do you think that was?

....
....
....
....

Are there any action steps you wish you had taken but didn't?

....
....
....
....

Are there any action steps you'd like to take more often?

....
....
....
....

Review & Reflect Week 6

Are there any other action steps you would like to add to the list? Please list them here:

....
....
....
....

Which action steps (they can be examples from the book or your own) would you like to make a regular, daily practice in your life to support your desire to be Emotionally Intelligent in Christ going forward? Please select at least three:

1. ....
2. ....
3. ....
4. ....
5. ....

Pray about the actions you listed above and would like to intentionally commit to, going forward. Who can help you stay accountable to them? Ask God to help you follow through with these now and commit your spiritual practice to Him.

....
....
....
....

Day 4
MEMORY VERSES

REVIEW:

Take some time to prayerfully review all of the *Memory Verses* you memorized over the course of the last five weeks. You can find them listed at the beginning of this week's lessons on page 204.

REFLECT:

As you reread these, which ones stand out to you?

....
....
....
....
....

Choose one that particularly supports your ability to discern and manage your emotions and behaviors in a way that honors God by loving others well, as Jesus did. Reflect on what it means to you here:

....
....
....
....
....
....
....

One by one, go through each of your memory verses and try to recite them by memory. Have you retained them? How did you do?

....
....
....
....
....
....
....

Select three of the five memory verses to commit to memory for the long haul. Practice them several times.

Call a friend and have them quiz you on each of these three verses. Then tell them what one of them means to you and why you are memorizing them in the first place.

Are there any memory verses you would like to intentionally commit to memorizing, going forward? If so, list them here:

How will you go about doing this? What time will you set aside for this? Where will you be? Who will hold you accountable? Please be as specific as possible.

Day 5
TO SUM IT UP

REVIEW:

Take some time to prayerfully review all of the *To Sum It Up* sections you have read over the course of the last five weeks.

REFLECT:

As you reread these, which ones stand out to you?

....
....
....
....
....

Which of these summary points would you like to spend additional time reflecting on? Why?

....
....
....
....
....

What is one aspect of God's character that has really been highlighted for you in the course of this study?

....
....
....
....
....
....

What is one aspect of your personality that has been highlighted for you in the course of this study?

....
....
....
....

Is there one area of your life where you would like to trust God more? What is it? Call or meet with a mentor or friend and share this with them. Then commit it to the Lord in prayer together.

....
....
....
....

If you were to summarize what you learned in this study into three main points, which ones would you choose? What are the main takeaways for you? Why do they stand out? Reflect on them here:

1. ....
2. ....
3. ....

....
....
....
....
....
....

Finally, take some time to thank God for all He's taught you over the course of the last six weeks. Thank Him for all He has already done and for all He is yet to do in and through you. Commit to an attitude of eager expectation as you learn to increasingly rely on Him in all of your interactions. Thank Him for maturing you and increasing your emotional intelligence in Him. Ask Him to solidify all of the lessons you have learned and apply them regularly in your Christ Encounters.

EIC STUDY GUIDE CONCLUSION

We hope this study has helped you understand yourself, your reactions, behaviors, and motivations better, so from now on you will be able to respond to the Christ Encounters God brings your way more and more thoughtfully with the love of Christ. We believe that an emotionally mature body of Christ will shine a brighter light into the world, be a more faithful witness, build healthier Christian communities, and establish more lifegiving Christ Connections with others.

As we operate out of Christ-in-us, our witness will be stronger, more consistent, and more compelling—not to mention that our lives will be more aligned with God's will and therefore more fulfilling. Loving well is a blessed way to live.

As you look back over the past 6-weeks, we hope you will find that the exercises and reflections in this book have not just improved your interactions with others but have also enhanced your relationship with God and yourself. As Thomas À Kempis states (EIC, p. 199), "Judging and analyzing ourselves, we always work to our own advantage."

Our hope is that the lessons you have learned over the past 6-weeks will equip you for ever-improving relationships with others, ongoing personal growth, and an ever-closer walk with our risen Savior, the author and originator of deep, life-transforming connections.

Connecting Hearts in Him,

Estella, Lauren, and Rich

For more information about the Emotional Intelligence in Christ Project please visit us at:
EmotionalIntelligenceinChrist.com

EMOTIONAL INTELLIGENCE IN CHRIST

5 STEPS TO LEAD AN EMOTIONAL INTELLIGENCE IN CHRIST 6-WEEK STUDY GROUP

SUGGESTED TIME: 60 MINUTES

PREPARATION:	Group meets 6 times to reflect on learnings and explore personal applications gained from the daily messages for each of the 6-weeks. Encourage one another.
1ST STEP	Check in with the group for prayer requests or identify how each member is doing with a quick check in statement. Philippians 2:4 *Do nothing out of selfish ambition or vain conceit. Rather, in humility value others above yourselves, 4 not looking to your own interests but each of you to the interests of the others.*
2ND STEP	Prepare in Prayer using the scripture verse for the week. *"Dear God, what is in these scriptures for me today which will remind my soul of what it already knows. Open the door to my heart and move my mind, emotions, and behaviors. Expand my ability to trust in you more today than yesterday."*

3ʳᵈ STEP	Reflect on what captured the group members' attention as you work through each lesson for the week.	
	Write down theme thoughts, *short phrases, which capture the group members reflections and discuss.*	
	For example: *"Do not conform to the pattern of this world but be transformed by the renewing of your mind"* (**Romans 12:2**). Theme Thought: Step away from the world: power; possessions; popularity and allow God to transform my thinking. Invite the group to write 1–3 theme thoughts that want to integrate into their daily walk with Jesus.	
4ᵗʰ STEP	Discuss the main take-a-ways that group members feel support Emotional Intelligence in Christ transformation.	
	Explore group insights on emotions and behaviors that either honor God or not. Continue the discussion on how these behaviors model the love of God for self and others. Explore solutions with the power of the Holy Spirit.	
	Luke 10:27 *He answered, "'Love the Lord your God with all your heart and with all your soul and with all your strength and with all your mind' and, 'Love your neighbor as yourself.'*	
5ᵗʰ STEP	Apply the EIC Method to help activate Emotional Intelligence in Christ.	
	Guide the group to use the EIC Method as described at the end of each daily lesson. Facilitate the sharing of encounters, identified behaviors, and how to course correct with the Holy Spirit. Use the scriptures covered in the lesson studied to encourage and build up individuals in the group.	
	Tie together the learnings gained in the group discussion with the definition of Emotional Intelligence in Christ: *The Activation of the Holy Spirit within you to discern and manage personal emotions and behaviors in a way that honors God by loving others well as Jesus did.* Pray in desired emotional and behavioral shifts expressed by the group.	

MEET THE EIC TEAM

Estella Chavous, EdD

Dr. Estella Chavous is an educator, communicator, course developer, global marketer, and well-being consultant. She is currently a global DEIW lead for AVEVA based in the Netherlands, an Adjunct Professor at UMass Global University, an Inside Timer Meditation Trainer, and a published author. Estella has significant professional experience in education, sales, and marketing, working in strategic leadership positions for Fortune 500 companies, including Abbott, Amgen, and Bristol Myers-Squibb. She has built and led effective teams throughout her career, designed and implemented successful strategies, and developed and managed diverse programs enabling the transformational process. As the co-founder of StrategicLadies, Dr. Estella provides personal, family, and corporate training and consulting in all aspects of well-being. She focuses on mindful meditation and contemplative prayer based on her relationship with Christ. Estella is the creator of the Christ-filled assessment booklet, co-author of an Amazon best-selling book, "Let Meditation Mend you, and the Emotional Intelligence In Christ book. She is also a co-host for the Mindful Media Show and co-founder of Edge God.

LAUREN E. MILLER, M.Ed, CSC, PCC

Lauren E. Miller, is first and foremost a follower of Jesus Christ with a passion for God's Holy Word and ministry. She accepted Jesus as her Lord and Savior at 17 years old and has worked in youth and adult ministries for over 30 years. With her love for God and people she launched her company in 2008 and serves the growth and development of people entrusted to her care. Education and Certifications include: Executive Coach, ICF-PCC (International Coach Federation) certified, Master NLP and EFT Practitioner and holds an WTF 2nd Degree Black Belt. She holds a Masters in Adult Education with a Certification in Human

Resources Development. Through God's mercy, grace, and strength, she has personally conquered two of life's top stressors at the same time, advanced cancer and divorce. Lauren is an SME in stress management, coaching youth and adults. Award-Winning Author: *Hearing His Whisper: With every storm Jesus Comes Too; 99 Things You Want to Know Before Stressing Out; Stop Letting the World Be the Boss of You: 25 Solutions to Refresh Your Identity In Christ; Emotional Intelligence In Christ*. She is a motivational speaker and HRD trainer, Lauren facilitates fun process driven programs. She is the co-founder and co-host of EdgeGodIn.com and it's podcast. Happily remarried, Lauren enjoys her gift of life in Colorado with her loving husband, three grown children and two grandchildren.

Richard Cummins, MAOL, CFRE

With more than twenty-years of senior leadership and c-suite experience, Rich is a life- long learner who is passionate about developing people and organizations while cultivating cultures built on relationships, service, and excellence. Currently, Rich serves as the Chief Operating Officer of Life Action Ministries, an organization dedicated to igniting movements of authentic Christianity. Rich has evidenced God's great provision in the organizations that he has served and with the people that he has invested in. He has a diverse background and leadership experience in the marketplace, military, and with Christ-centered nonprofit organizations and institutions of higher education. Rich finds purpose in helping other leaders optimize their leadership through self-awareness and relational effectiveness. He has earned a Master of Arts in Organizational Leadership at Huntington University, an Advanced Executive Coaching credential from the Townsend Institute, and is a Certified Fundraising Executive with CFRE International. Rich also serves his church as an ordained minister. Rich's favorite moments involve spending time with his wife, Danielle, and five amazing children traveling, fishing, and hiking. He really enjoys conversations about Jesus and leadership.

www.ingramcontent.com/pod-product-compliance
Lightning Source LLC
Chambersburg PA
CBHW061153010526
44118CB00027B/2957